SHELLY PAGLIAI

QUILTING *for* HIRE

START YOUR OWN LONGARM OR CUSTOM QUILTMAKING BUSINESS

Vision, Business Plan, Tools & Supplies, Branding, Marketing & More

C&T PUBLISHING

Publisher: Amy Barrett-Daffin

Creative Director: Gailen Runge

Acquisitions Editor: Roxane Cerda

Managing Editor: Liz Aneloski

Editor: Katie Van Amburg

Technical Editor: Debbie Rodgers

Cover/Book Designer: April Mostek

Production Coordinator: Tim Manibusan

Production Editor: Alice Mace Nakanishi

Illustrator: Casey Dukes

Production Assistant: Gabriel Martinez

Published by C&T Publishing, Inc., P.O. Box 1456, Lafayette, CA 94549

Library of Congress Cataloging-in-Publication Data

Names: Pagliai, Shelly, 1962- author.

Title: Quilting for hire : start your own longarm or custom quiltmaking business : vision, business plan, tools & supplies, branding, marketing & more / Shelly Pagliai.

Description: Lafayette, CA : C&T Publishing, [2022]

Identifiers: LCCN 2021031674 | ISBN 9781644030868 (trade paperback) | ISBN 9781644030875 (ebook)

Subjects: LCSH: Quilting shops--Management. | New business enterprises--Management. | Small business--Management. | Quilting--Vocational guidance.

Classification: LCC TT835.5 .P34 2022 | DDC 746.46068--dc23

LC record available at https://lccn.loc.gov/2021031674

Printed in the USA

10 9 8 7 6 5 4 3 2 1

dedication

TO GRANDPA HYDE ... You always wanted me to be a business-woman, but I wanted to be an artist. Somehow, I've managed to do both. I hope you're proud of me.

TO DADDY ... Thanks for always encouraging me to be an artist. I'll always love you most.

TO MY COWBOY ... I would never have gotten this far or done this much without your help, love, support, and encouragement. All I can say is thank you and I love you, even though it's not enough. And no, I have no idea what we're having for supper.

acknowledgments

You never get through something like this all alone, and I sure have my share of kind folks to thank for helping me. Thank you to ...

- My Cowboy, for everything.

- Victoria Findlay Wolfe, for trusting me, encouraging me, and keeping me from being lazy.

- Edie McGinnis, for saving me from myself.

- Karen McTavish, Melanie Miller-Thurnau, Laurie Love, Becky Collis, Karyn Dornemann, Ida Larsen, Angela Steiner, Melinda Masten, and Keith Morrissey, for being so kind and patient and answering all sorts of questions for me.

- Dan Terrell, former owner of Nolting Manufacturing, for selling me my first longarm machine, and the current support staff of Nolting, who take good care of Ivy and keep us up and running.

- All the folks at C&T Publishing, especially my design team.

contents

Foreword 6   **Introduction 9**

PART 1 **QUILTING FOR HIRE**   **11**

CH 1 **What You Should Know Before You Take the Leap** 12

Questions to Ask Yourself 13

Things to Consider 21

CH 2 **First Steps** 25

Define Your Vision 27

Quilt Business Research 31

Set Yourself Up 36

Craft the Perfect Business Plan 43

Create an Action Plan 55

CH 3 **Hanging Out Your Shingle** 57

Location 58

Equipment 62

Tools and Supplies 72

Build Your Brand 74

Establish Your Online Presence 77

CH 4 **Setting Customer Expectations** 81

What Services Will You Provide? 82

Find Your Customers 84

Paperwork 88

Reaching Agreement 94

Shipping and Handling 99

Personal Touches 102

CH 5 Making the Magic Happen 103

Setting Up Your Space 104

Scheduling 107

Organizing Your Time 111

Doing the Work 117

CH 6 Money, Money, Money 122

Setting Prices 123

Accounting Concerns 128

Taxes 130

Financial Concerns 132

Insurance 134

CH 7 Marketing 139

Increasing Your Audience 140

Making Connections 143

Advertising 145

Media 146

Social Media 148

CH 8 Expanding 154

Adding More Equipment 155

Hiring Help 155

Teaching Others 158

Renting Time 161

Designing Patterns and Tools 161

PART 2 PIECING AND CUSTOM QUILTMAKING FOR HIRE 163

CH 9 Getting Started 164

Finding Your Niche 165

Do Your Research 167

Develop Your Product 168

Spread the Word 170

CH 10 Getting Set Up 172

Equipment and Tools 173

Organizing Your Space 175

Adding Quiltmaking to Your Schedule 180

CH 11 Money, Contracts, and Help—Oh My! 182

The Quiltmaking Agreement 183

Commission Work Prices 185

Paperwork/Contracts 194

Hiring Help and Adding Equipment 201

An Extra-Special Finish 202

You Did It! 204   Resources 205   About the Author 208

foreword

I met Shelly in the late summer of 2009. I was part of a Pay-It-Forward challenge on my blog. You had to make something for the next person whose name was on the list, and I got Shelly. I followed her blog, read about her Cowboy, and made her a table runner from cutting up my old duvet cover! I had posted on my blog that I would be going to Houston for the International Quilt Festival, and she responded, asking if we should meet in Houston—she and the Cowboy would also be going to see her quilt hanging in the show. I was quick to say yes! I remember calling her from the floor of Festival trying to locate her in the sea of people. She said, "I'm with my Cowboy, you'll spot him first," and sure enough, there they were. We chatted, laughed, and connected from that moment on.

Around that time, I had put out a call for quilters to make pieced house blocks for a community quilt project I was working on for homeless families transitioning back into homes in the New York City area. I was going to make a few quilts to donate to them and Shelly said, "Well, I just got a longarm machine, I could quilt some of them to practice." Those quilts came back quilted so beautifully, and she certainly got to practice! I ended up making about 75 quilts, many quilted by Shelly and other longarmers donating their time. Those first quilts were auctioned off and raised around $30,000 for the organization. That call turned into about a 3,000-quilt drive, and every family moving into new housing through the program received a new quilt. This experience included my passion for making, sharing, and giving. It connected me to Shelly and other quilters in the quilting world, and I found my community. Since those first collaborations together, Shelly and I have never looked back. AND TOGETHER, OUR WORK HAS GROWN OVER THE YEARS INTO BUSINESSES, ALONG WITH THE STEADY COLLABORATION PROCESS WE BOTH LOVE.

HISTORICALLY, FOR MANY WOMEN, QUILTING HAS BEEN NOT ONLY A HOBBY BUT ALSO A BUSINESS—from mail-order patterns to kit quilts to hiring hand quilters to finish the quilts. So it makes perfect sense for longarming to be an exciting business choice—for all people! I remember feeling scared about letting someone quilt for me, then getting the quilt back and learning so much from the way it was quilted. I could look for a detail that I could emulate on my next quilt. Each time I'd make a quilt, I'd try some new design. Shortly after my first book was published, I purchased a longarm for myself, and later another longarm, and I had so much fun learning how to manage the machines. Yet, I quickly found that my patience for longarming was not to be part of my business plan. More than once, I quilted halfway through a quilt, then ended up taking it off the frame and sending it to Shelly to finish. I traveled too much to be able to keep up, but I knew longarm quilting was where Shelly was focusing her business. It was a perfect fit.

I've watched Shelly and her business grow, and I am constantly blown away by her work. The conversations I have with Shelly often include the questions: *What can we try now? What does this need? What do you think it should look like?* I have found the duality of working together to be much more compelling than working alone, and I like that it continues to add another part of the story to the quilt. I recall us having a weeklong conversation of about ten different ideas I had for quilting on my *Cascade* quilt from my book *Modern Quilt Magic*. I felt bad because I thought I must have completely overwhelmed Shelly with information. Yet, I got back a quilt that incorporated everything I had given her—and it is to die for! Other times, I call her in the middle of constructing a quilt, and I point out to her where I'm focusing my attention. We talk about what else we could do with the quilting to get the final result I'm looking for—maybe it's not in the construction, maybe it is in the quilting. Oftentimes it is in the quilting.

I know we did it well when we get comments on our collaboration quilts: "Great quilt! But that quilting is phenomenal!"

That. That is the experience Shelly brings to the table.

I feel lucky to have worked with Shelly over these past eleven to twelve years, to have her to bounce ideas off as we both built our successful businesses. Over the years, we have discussed together how our businesses ebb and flow. We brainstorm and share ideas to figure out what's next.

Shelly is very aware of her market and her brand, and she has learned how to best schedule work that fits her life and keeps her customers happy. This experience of balance is the key wisdom you will get from this book. Shelly will guide you through the basics of a quilting business and get you thinking about questions you may not have thought of, so you can keep a full schedule of quilts booked out months ahead for your success. Getting help with taxes and bookkeeping or wholesale ordering all help to fulfill your business goals.

Shelly's humor and knowledge—something I love about her—will keep you in good hands as you read through the book. This guide is something that Shelly and I wish we had had when we started our businesses! Lucky you!

I'm also happy that longarmers are here to stay. That means I can sell my two machines and focus on making the quilt tops I love to make! I can make quilts together with you fabulous future longarm stars and continue new collaborations with Shelly for a long time to come.

~ **VICTORIA FINDLAY WOLFE**
International award–winning quilter; author of *15 Minutes of Play— Improvisational Quilts, Double Wedding Ring Quilts—Traditions Made Modern, Modern Quilt Magic,* and *Victoria Findlay Wolfe's Playing with Purpose* (all with C&T Publishing); **designer; teacher; and friend**

introduction

IF YOU HAVE A LONGARM QUILTING MACHINE, YOU'VE BEEN QUILTING AS A HOBBY, AND YOU'VE BEEN TOYING WITH THE IDEA OF USING YOUR LONGARM TO QUILT TOPS FOR OTHER QUILTERS AS A BUSINESS, THEN THIS BOOK IS FOR YOU.

If you're thinking of purchasing a longarm machine with the intention of quilting tops for other quilters, then this book is definitely for you.

If you're thinking ... the world doesn't need any more longarm quilters because there are already so many, then *stop that*! Professional machine quilters are in high demand—you can be one of them. There is plenty of room in this business for you. Besides, you will not be exactly like any of the others out there.

> "The world needs that special gift that only you have." ~ MARIE FORLEO

••• This is a book of questions. It's chock-full of questions to ask yourself—and I'm not going to provide you with all the answers. It's intended to make you think, plan, and figure out this whole business thing in a way that will work for *you*. Your business will not look like anyone else's business, and that is just fine. Being unique is good!

You'll want to think everything through based on *your* own situation before you begin. These questions and the information I am offering should help prepare you for the road to success.

***Outside the United States?** If you don't live in the United States, your business setup requirements may be different, so make sure to do your research on starting a business in your country as needed.*

QUILTING IS FUN ... THE BUSINESS OF QUILTING, NOT SO MUCH.
Creative people just want to create and not have to deal with the
business end of things; but to be successful, you can't ignore that
business part. My goal with this book is for it to be interesting and
thought-provoking.

Treat it like a workbook, and work your way through each chapter.
There are forms to help you throughout the book, and some of them
are available as downloads, so you can download and print them as
many times as you need.

Downloads: tinyurl.com/11441-forms-download

If you need to ask questions from an expert (for instance, an accountant, insurance agent, or tax specialist), take the time to seek them out.
Don't rush through it too quickly. Go over it more than once, and keep
adding new information and ideas to what you've already come up
with. After you've been in business for a while, revisit this book again
and you might come up with some new ideas as your business grows.

> I can't tell you it will be easy. Building a business
> takes time, and you won't become a Rock Star Quilter
> overnight—but having a plan and being organized
> from the get-go will alleviate a lot of stress.

I wish I had had a book like this when I first started my business; I
wish I had known all the right questions to ask. There are so many
things that I didn't think through. My hope is that this book can spare
you all the mistakes I've made, and you can start out further ahead
without having to figure out everything on your own.

Pretend you're sitting with me having a chat. You've told me that you
want to start a longarm business, and I'm asking you all these questions. What would you tell me?

POUR US A CUPPA ... I'M READY FOR YOUR ANSWERS. ARE YOU?

PART 1

QUILTING FOR HIRE

CHAPTER 1

what you should know before you take the leap

IF YOU ARE CONSIDERING QUILTING FOR HIRE, OR IF YOU'RE ALREADY QUILTING FOR HIRE BUT WISH TO GROW YOUR BUSINESS, THERE ARE A LOT OF THINGS TO TAKE INTO CONSIDERATION. In this chapter is a list of questions you need to ask yourself. Think over your answers carefully, and be brutally honest with yourself—because no one else will be as brutally honest with you as you can and should be in this case.

While this list of questions may seem daunting, and, in some cases, difficult to answer, it is not meant to be discouraging. Quite the opposite, in fact! It's meant to make you think seriously about what you're preparing to undertake, so you don't get blindsided after you start. You, being the smart cookie you are, will have considered all these things beforehand, and you'll be prepared for any situation that arises and tries to derail you. You can do this!

QUESTIONS TO ASK YOURSELF

Are you prepared to be an entrepreneur?

More than once, I've heard it said:

"You will work longer, harder hours for yourself in your own business than you ever will for someone else."

And it's true. You have a vested interest in making your own business succeed. You are the boss, with only yourself to answer to, so your business is always on your mind. Because you're not limited to regular working hours, it can be physically and emotionally exhausting. Can you handle it?

I've been known to snap wide awake in the middle of the night, either with an exciting new idea, panic over a deadline, the feeling that I've forgotten something important, or guilt over not getting enough done. I've also worked 20- to 22-hour days to meet deadlines, along with skipping much-needed meals and showers, simply because I haven't been able to spare the time to do those things! (Good thing I work alone at home, right?)

YOU WILL FACE QUANDARIES ABOUT TAKING ON MORE WORK OR TURNING DOWN CERTAIN JOBS, BECAUSE IT FEELS BAD TO TURN MONEY AWAY, BUT THEN AGAIN, SOMETIMES YOU SIMPLY CAN'T TAKE ON ONE MORE THING OR YOU'LL SNAP. You need to know yourself and learn how to keep the balance. I have definitely learned that sleepless nights are no fun, and regular meals and showers are a good thing! But also keep in mind that—even if you plan a balanced schedule—unexpected things can come up that can throw your whole schedule into a tailspin, such as getting sick or having a family emergency (or in my case, having to bottle-feed baby goats or deal with the ranch crisis du jour), and in order to deliver on what you've promised, an occasional hectic period will occur. Will this bother you?

What are some things that go on in your life that might derail you temporarily? How can you prepare your business so that it can weather the rough periods and still survive?

_____

_____

_____

_____

_____

_____

_____

_____

Do you have what it takes to run your own business?

Are you disciplined enough to put in the hours required to make your business a success? Can you be your own boss? You'll have to answer to yourself, but you'll also have to answer to your customers, and you are the only one responsible for doing what you say you'll do. You're also the only one to blame when things go wrong. Are you prepared for that?

YOU WON'T HAVE A REGULAR PAYCHECK LIKE YOU WOULD IF YOU WERE WORKING FOR SOMEONE ELSE. Cash flow issues can be very stressful, sometimes expenses will outweigh the income, and you may start to think in terms of "How many quilts am I going to have to quilt to pay for that?" Equipment breakdowns, customers who are slow to pay, overhead expenses, cost of supplies, underestimation of the time it takes to complete a job—all these things can cause extra worry, and you need to be prepared to deal with it.

*

How many hours do you want to devote to your business each week?

_____

How many hours can you realistically devote to your business each week?

_____

Is it a side gig? Or are you going full time?

_____

Can you put a plan in place to make it through the slow times or the unexpected expenses?

_____

_____

_____

_____

_____

_____

Will turning your hobby into a business make you hate your hobby?

If you're currently only quilting part time, or as a hobby, will transitioning to quilting full time and running a quilting business be an absolute dream for you? Or will it make you hate your hobby and burn out?

I personally would be quilting every spare minute of my day even if it wasn't my full-time job, so having it as my full-time job is truly a dream come true. But if that doesn't sound fun to you, and the siren song of other activities is constantly pulling at you, maybe consider staying part time, rather than let the business make you hate quilting. Only you can decide how much is too much and whether you can spend that kind of time doing it.

What are some nonquilting activities that you regularly spend time doing and don't want to give up? Can you figure out ways to fit it all in?

_____   _____

_____   _____

_____   _____

_____   _____

_____   _____

_____   _____

_____   _____

_____   _____

Can you keep yourself motivated?

Will you be okay with waking up day after day and quilting for other people? Or does the thought of that bore you to tears?

EVERYONE IS INSPIRED TO STAY MOTIVATED BY DIFFERENT THINGS. FINDING WHAT WORKS FOR YOU WILL BE KEY TO STICKING WITH IT AND MOVING FORWARD. I'll cover various ways to stay motivated in Chapter 5 (see How to Stay Motivated, page 118)—but know that losing your motivation can be a very real thing that impacts your business, so be prepared to deal with it.

Can you keep your work time and family time separated?

This is one of the most difficult parts of working at home. It's easy to succumb to the pull of household tasks that need doing, so you might spend too much time at that. Conversely, you might become a workaholic, ignoring the family and household tasks too much.

Will your family understand the difference between your work time and your family time? If you work at home, your family may not respect that you have definite working hours, and think that you are available whenever they need you, for whatever they need you for. And while this is true for important things (which is one of the benefits of working from home), it can also mean a lot of interruptions for not-so-important things. You have to establish the ground rules with them, to protect your working time, but you also need to balance that out with the right amount of family time. Sometimes it's not an easy thing to do.

One way to determine whether you are balancing your family/work time effectively is to keep a time log for a few days. For more on this, see Time Log: A Week in the Life... (page 111), in Chapter 5.

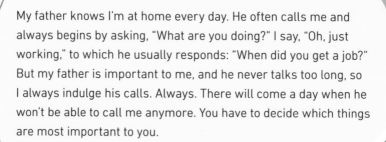

My father knows I'm at home every day. He often calls me and always begins by asking, "What are you doing?" I say, "Oh, just working," to which he usually responds: "When did you get a job?" But my father is important to me, and he never talks too long, so I always indulge his calls. Always. There will come a day when he won't be able to call me anymore. You have to decide which things are most important to you.

Are you physically able to stand at your machine for hours on end and do the work required?

Running a longarm machine is hard on your body. You can do a lot of things to make it ergonomically better, but even so, the hours required when it's your business can still be grueling. It's hard on your eyes, hands, back, feet, neck, shoulders, and legs. It can be exhausting, both physically and mentally. YOU NEED TO BE ABLE TO WITHSTAND THE TOLL IT MAY TAKE ON YOUR BODY.

Can you wear all the hats required to run a business?

Do you even want to?

IN ADDITION TO BEING AN ACTUAL QUILTER, THERE ARE MANY, MANY OTHER HATS THAT RUNNING YOUR OWN BUSINESS REQUIRES YOU TO WEAR. You will also need to be a bookkeeper, website administrator, social media manager, customer service representative, purchasing agent, shipping and receiving clerk, janitor, inventory control specialist, student, and technician, just to name a few. And this doesn't include the other possible hats you wear as a spouse, parent, housekeeper, caretaker, errand runner, and so on. How many hats are you willing to wear?

List below all the hats you might possibly have to wear (both business and personal) while running your own quilting business:

_____   _____   _____

_____   _____   _____

_____   _____   _____

_____   _____   _____

_____   _____   _____

Do you have the business skills you need?

ARE YOU WILLING TO DEVELOP THE ONES YOU DON'T HAVE? OR HIRE THEM OUT?

Are you an accountant? Can you do your own bookkeeping? Are you tech-savvy enough that you can build, manage, and update your own website? Will you have time for these things, and still be able to do as much quilting as you need to? What about having to learn new software? Manage your social media accounts? Repair your own machine if it breaks down?

You need to either have or build these skills, or hire someone who can do them for you, which could be money well spent, if it frees up your time and relieves the stress of having to do them yourself.

Referring back to your list of possible hats you need to wear while running your own business, make a list below of the skills you already have and the skills you need to either learn or hire out.

SKILLS I HAVE

_____

_____

_____

_____

_____

_____

_____

_____

_____

_____

_____

_____

_____

_____

_____

_____

SKILLS I NEED

_____

_____

_____

_____

_____

_____

_____

_____

_____

_____

_____

_____

_____

_____

_____

_____

THINGS TO CONSIDER

Can you effectively manage your time and your priorities?

Do you find yourself wasting time on things other than quilting, such as scrolling through social media or otherwise procrastinating? It's helpful to know yourself and when you do your best focused work and to schedule appropriate tasks to fit those times. I'll cover some tips for this in Chapter 5, with more about filling out a time log worksheet to get an idea of how you spend your time each week, so you can see where you can make adjustments to use your time more efficiently.

Can you work with customers and put their needs and wants above your own?

Most of your customers will have expected deadlines for when their quilt will be completed. Some may have urgent deadlines, but have no idea how your schedule works and expect the impossible. All your customers will have various requirements for how they want their quilts finished and how much they want to spend. You need to be ready to offer them options, including a variety of price points, and be clear about what your schedule is like.

••• Can you deal with the pressure of deadlines, when it may mean working extra hours in a short period of time? If you have an idea of how a quilt should be quilted, but the customer wants something you don't necessarily agree with, can you happily give them what they want? Are you ready to discuss different options with them? We discuss all of this in Chapter 4.

> **Can you do quality work that you're proud of, or do you need more practice and experience first?**

Sending shoddy workmanship out into the world results in bad press and is difficult to overcome. Be sure you are ready to do quality work, but on the other hand, don't think so poorly of your own work that you hesitate too long. We are always our own worst critics, but still, you want your work to represent you well, and bring in more customers.

TAKE TIME TO PRACTICE, EVEN AFTER YOU'VE BEGUN QUILTING FOR OTHERS. Take classes (either online or in person), read books on techniques, watch videos, study the quilting of those you admire, sketch and doodle when you can, and try out new things on quilts of your own, so you will be ready to do them for others with confidence in your skill.

I've been quilting for years, and I still learn something new on nearly every quilt. Don't be afraid to let your customers push you out of your comfort zone. Pressure shapes diamonds, and it can make you an even better quilter over time.

It has always seemed an unfortunate catch-22 that people won't hire you if you don't have experience, but you can't get experience if no one will hire you. If you're running your own business, you can give yourself the experience you need and then build up your clientele by showing your work and letting your reputation for quality work speak for you.

"Longarming: It ain't fer sissies." ~ **MY COWBOY**

Why?! **Why do you want to go into the business of quilting for hire?**
What are your reasons? This is important, because if you don't have a
strong enough "why," you may not be ready for this, and it's not good to
take a hobby you love and turn it into a failed business that makes you
miserable. You should write this down. ... I'll wait.

_____

_____

_____

**Can you think of a few pros and cons of going into the quilting for hire
business and working for yourself?** Jot down a few here. Which list is
bigger?

PROS	CONS
_____	_____
_____	_____
_____	_____
_____	_____
_____	_____

Here's my list:

PROS	CONS
I can't get fired.	Longer hours.
I can set my own schedule.	Variable cash flow.
I get to work from home ...	Distractions and interruptions.
... alone ...	I have to deal with everything myself, including the mundane.
... in my pajamas!	
I have a job I love.	

So, are you ready?

• • • As you've worked your way through this list of questions to ask yourself before deciding to start up a business of quilting for hire, I hope you've remembered to be very honest with yourself. If you don't have everything figured out just yet, don't be discouraged. You can work a lot of it out along the way.

There are many other things to take into consideration. Read on for more on these topics, along with a lot of other information to help you decide if it's right for you. I'm here to help you get started if you've already decided this is exactly what you want to do with your life. Let's go!

NOTES

CHAPTER 2

first steps

BEFORE YOU GET STARTED QUILTING FOR HIRE, YOU NEED TO HAVE A BIT OF A ROAD MAP AS TO WHERE YOU'RE HEADED. You don't have to have every little thing planned out, but you do need to have a pretty good idea of what you want your business to be like, and how you might like to grow it.

> *"If you fail to plan, you are planning to fail."*
> ~ **BENJAMIN FRANKLIN**

THERE ARE MANY THINGS THAT CAN CAUSE YOUR BUSINESS TO FAIL: the economy, less-than-stellar marketing, poor customer service, shoddy workmanship, lack of experience, lack of desire or motivation, or personal and family issues (such as poor health and other issues).

If you think that the actual quilting part is mostly what you'll be doing, head on back to Chapter 1 (Can you wear all the hats required to run a business?, page 19) and take a look at that list of hats you'll be wearing as a reminder that running a business is a lot of work in many areas.

It is normal to have doubts, but don't let the doubts keep you from getting started. You will probably never feel like you are completely ready, but if you work your way through this chapter, you can go ahead and take the plunge, and work out the kinks after you get started. If you build your business slowly, you'll have a better chance of succeeding than if you try to do it all right out of the gate. So do your research and conquer those fears as you follow your dream.

DEFINE YOUR VISION

What do you want your business to look like? Sit back with a cup of your favorite beverage and a notebook, and imagine in your head how your day-to-day will be. (And then remind yourself that most days will *not* be like this, but we can dream, right?)

Here are some questions to get you started.

Should you work from home or from an off-site studio?

Which is the better scenario for your particular situation? I go into more detail about this in Chapter 3, but do begin thinking about it now.

Are you going to quilt full time or part time?

Do you need to quilt full time to make more money? Or will you be quilting part time to supplement your current income? In Chapter 1, I asked you to estimate how many hours you will devote to your business each week. If you're ready to step into it full time, that's great. But if you don't want that, or you're not quite to that point, don't worry.

••• If you still have a "day job" that you're not willing to give up just yet, obviously you will only be able to quilt for others part time, but this could be in preparation for when the time comes that you can quit your day job and start quilting full time. By then, you will know if it's for you, you will have a customer base built up, and you will have a lot more experience under your belt. It'll be easy to step into it as a full-time job.

Or maybe you want to stay part time even after you give up your day job, simply for something to do and to make a little extra money, or because a part-time schedule works better for you and your particular situation.

"I am longarming part time as I also have a career as a chiropractor (that is also part time). I quilt all day Friday and Monday, and a lot over the weekends too, especially if I have a deadline for a customer's quilt."

~ KARYN DORNEMANN, OF KARYNQUILTS

What types of quilting will you do?

There are many different types of longarm quilters. Some only do computerized edge-to-edge quilting; some only do edge-to-edge quilting without a computerized machine; some only do custom quilting; some do a little bit of all of it. What do you want to do? What will you feel comfortable doing?

For more help in making this decision, check out What Services Will You Provide? (page 82), in Chapter 4.

Do you want to eventually expand?

* How big do you want your business to grow?

* Do you want to reach a certain point and hold steady?

* Do you want to work your way through different skill levels as you gain experience?

* Do you want to pick a level and just remain there and work steadily in that type of quilting?

* Do you want to add some other services to your line-up?

* Do you want to hire help?

Seriously, there is only so much one person can do, so you will need to decide where your tipping point is. If you're spreading yourself too thin, your business will suffer in several areas, so think this over carefully. If you get going and see that the next level will be too much, you will need to decide which direction to steer your business in order to keep your sanity (or your spouse!).

In addition to offering different levels of quilting (see What Services Will You Provide?, page 82), there are other ways of expanding your quilting business, and I'll cover those in Chapter 8.

BUT THIS LEADS DIRECTLY TO THE NEXT QUESTION. ...

What do you want to be known for?

Do you want to be known for ...

→ ... your quick turnaround times?

→ ... your sharply executed computerized designs?

→ ... your wide selection of available pantograph or edge-to-edge designs?

→ ... your kick-ass custom quilting?

→ ... your attention to detail?

→ ... your gorgeous heirloom quilting?

→ ... your fun, modern style?

→ ... your fantastic feathers?

→ ... your ability to interpret (and skillfully execute) just what a quilt top is asking for?

→ ... the wonderful tools or patterns you've invented?

YOU NEED TO DECIDE WHAT KIND OF QUILTING YOU WANT TO DO THE MOST OF AND BE KNOWN FOR AND BE WILLING TO DO IT OVER AND OVER AND OVER AGAIN.

I'll also cover some ways to make sure you are emphasizing your particular talents to your potential customer base in Chapter 7.

QUILT BUSINESS RESEARCH

You will need to do a fair bit of research in several different areas before you start your business. And don't let it stop there. You need to keep doing research throughout the life of your business, so you can stay current with the industry and change gears, if necessary.

Where do you start?

Well, first, talk to your family and friends. Will you have a support system for your endeavor? There will be some who are excited for you and willing to help. There will be some who are naysayers and dream squelchers, too. Sort them carefully. Surround yourself with those who will provide encouragement, support, and positivity; try to avoid the negative voices and the downers. Don't let anyone tell you that you can't do this.

IT WILL BE REALLY GREAT IF YOU HAVE AT LEAST ONE OR TWO CLOSE SUPPORTERS OR A MENTOR THAT YOU CAN BOUNCE IDEAS OFF OF AS YOU GO THROUGH THE STARTUP PROCESS. List a couple people that you feel you can confide in and depend on for honest support, or ask reliable advice from.

1. _____

2. _____

Next, I hope you like to read ... because I'm going to tell you to do a lot of it. I've included an extensive Resources (page 205) section in this book that I hope you will refer to. But here are some important suggestions to get you started.

U.S. SMALL BUSINESS ADMINISTRATION

Use the resources offered by the Small Business Administration. They have a wealth of information online. They also help fund Small Business Development Centers across the country, where you can find local help in person. These are usually located on college or university campuses, but use the locator on the SBA's website to find the one nearest you.

••• Do spend a good amount of time looking through what the SBA offers online. I can't emphasize this enough. You can find answers to a lot of your questions right there. And, if you intend to go visit one of the SBDC offices, and speak to someone in person, you want to have a written list of good questions to ask and get answers for. Don't just walk in without knowing what you want to ask them. You'll only be wasting your time and theirs.

YOU MIGHT ALSO CHECK TO SEE IF YOUR AREA HAS A LOCAL CHAMBER OF COMMERCE THAT CAN PROVIDE YOU WITH SOME INFORMATION. If they're an active and helpful Chamber, it might even behoove you to become a member to take advantage of their help with promoting your business locally.

"*That word:* behoove. *It just doesn't get used near enough, does it?*"

~ AMANDA JEAN NYBERG, OF CRAZY MOM QUILTS

ATTEND QUILT SHOWS

To begin with, go to quilt shows to study the quilting that is being done. You will get a lot of ideas about the type(s) of quilting services you might like to offer. If you happen to meet any of the quilters themselves, you can ask them questions and make some connections.

Later on, you can go to quilt shows to pass out your own business information and network with other quilters and a lot of potential customers. Local and national shows will both provide you with opportunities, so go when you can.

JOIN A QUILT GUILD

THIS IS A GREAT WAY TO SEE THE WORK OF OTHERS, MAKE NEW QUILTING FRIENDS, GAIN NEW CUSTOMERS, AND SHARE YOUR WORK. Check your local area to see what's available. There are even guilds specifically for longarm quilters, which is even better!

ATTEND A QUILTING TRADE SHOW

Twice a year, a quilting industry trade show called Quilt Market takes place. While you need specific credentials to be allowed to attend, if you are already in business, you will be able to easily provide these credentials. If you are not yet in business, you may need to wait until you're more established. However, if you can get in, I encourage you to go at least once. It's a fantastic place to gather all sorts of information; see all the latest machines, tools, and gadgets; network with like-minded folks; make industry contacts; and even take business classes. You will come away with your head spinning full of new ideas, inspiration, and possibly some new customers.

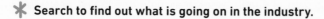

USE THE INTERNET

* Search to find out what is going on in the industry.

* Join Facebook groups to watch, learn, and discuss all things quilting. Many groups are devoted specifically to longarm quilters, where you can ask questions, get answers, contribute to discussions, get help from, and give help to other quilters just like yourself.

* Learn about trends and styles (use Instagram, Facebook, Pinterest, digital magazines, ...).

* Study the quilting of others on their websites or on social media.

* Find suppliers.

* Take classes.

* Listen to podcasts.

* Watch videos.

* Look up business information (on branding, on business plans, on marketing, on motivation, on planning and goal-setting ... it's all out there just waiting to be read by you).

* Use the information you find to brainstorm ideas of your own. Don't forget to write them down, even if they seem silly. You can weed through them later.

AND DON'T EVER STOP DOING THESE THINGS. Build time into your schedule for self-improvement and professional development. Always keep studying what's going on in your industry so you can keep improving. And if you ever find your motivation fading, this is a great way to jump-start it!

QUILTING FOR HIRE

SPEND TIME AT THE BOOKSTORE OR LIBRARY

Browse the business section; check out books that might help you. Browse books for topics that might be of help as you're getting started. Check out all the quilting magazines to look at the quilts inside and read pertinent articles.

Once you have your business up and running, keep on reading so that you can continue to improve. Never stop learning!

BE A SPY

ALWAYS BE LOOKING AT WHAT OTHERS ARE DOING AND LEARN FROM THEM. Not so you can copy them, but so you can learn new things to try that will push you to develop your own skills even further. You can see the work of others at quilt shows, guild meetings, trunk shows, lectures, workshops, or online on Facebook, Instagram, or Pinterest. Try new tools, ask questions, get ideas, make new friends, and network.

You can collect ideas from looking at what others in this same profession are doing, such as the types of quilting they do, photos of their studio spaces, their machines and equipment, and the services they offer.

But... do *not* get caught up in comparing yourself to others. Just don't. There is only one you, and there is plenty of room for you in this industry—don't let anyone convince you that there isn't.

SET YOURSELF UP

BEFORE YOU CAN HANG OUT YOUR SHINGLE, YOU NEED TO ATTEND TO A FEW LEGAL AND BUSINESS MATTERS. A lot of good information can be found online about the forms you may need to file, and a trip to your local county courthouse or city hall might do you a world of good. Consult with a lawyer and/or an accountant before you go, so that you can make sure you're asking all the right questions and not leaving out something important.

The rules and regulations of your own city, county, and state (and even your HOA, if you have one) will vary depending on where you live, but here are some general things you'll need to take care of:

Check Local Zoning Regulations

••• You will need to check with your local Planning and Zoning Commission (and HOA or landlord, if you have them) to see if it's legal to operate a business from your home. Most cities have zoning laws to keep residential areas separate from commercial and industrial areas, so they remain quieter and cleaner. Your local zoning board can tell you if it's legal to operate a quilting business from your home or not. If not, then you may need to apply for a zoning variance, which may require you to pay a fee. If you are not having an excess of clients coming to your home or creating too much obvious business activity at your residence, you should find it easy to get approved.

Choose a Business Entity

There are many types of business entities, but the two most common for the business of quilting for hire are the Sole Proprietorship and the Limited Liability Company (LLC). I describe these two below, but I recommend that you consult a lawyer and/or an accountant if you are unsure which one is right for you.

SOME QUESTIONS YOU MIGHT ASK YOUR ACCOUNTANT:

What are the tax effects of each type of entity, and which type of entity is best for me?

What taxes do I need to plan for?

When do I pay these taxes?

How do I pay these taxes?

SOLE PROPRIETORSHIP

A Sole Proprietorship is the simplest and most common type of business entity, especially for a small business operating at home. It's easy to start: no special forms to fill out or file, taxes are simpler than for an LLC, and you shouldn't need legal help to get going. You are your own boss, and you get all the profits, but it also means that you are personally liable for all business debts and have unlimited legal liability.

LIMITED LIABILITY COMPANY (LLC)

Becoming an LLC usually requires certain forms to be filed, and although it can be fairly easy, you will probably want the help of a lawyer or an accountant to make sure you've covered all your bases. The main advantage of choosing to become an LLC is the unlimited liability protection it affords, if you think you will need that type of protection.

Choose a Name for Your Business

Your business will need a name! This may not be as easy as it sounds, although you've probably been mulling this over for a while. Once you name your business, it'll be something you'll have to live with for a long time, so make sure you like it! You also need it to be something that is easy to pronounce and that fits with your brand (see Build Your Brand, page 74).

MAKE SURE THE NAME YOU CHOOSE IS NOT ALREADY TAKEN. You can do a quick search online to see if it's already in use somewhere. Also check Facebook, Instagram, Twitter, and Pinterest to make sure your name is unique and not already in use.

My business, Prairie Moon Quilts, is named after our cattle ranch, Prairie Moon Ranch. Since I did not use my full name as part of my business name, I had to register a fictitious name with the state of Missouri. It has to be renewed every five years.

If I were to have named my business Shelly Pagliai's Quilting Emporium, then I would not have needed to file a fictitious name form because I have included my full name. But if I had called it Shelly's Custom Quilting or Pagliai's Professional Quilting, I would still need to register a fictitious name, since the name of my business doesn't include my full name. Be sure and check with your own state to see if these same rules apply. When you file this form, the state will also alert you to whether the name is already taken, so you can change it to something unique.

YOUR BUSINESS WILL ALSO NEED A PHYSICAL ADDRESS FOR MAILING PURPOSES, AND YOU CAN DECIDE IF YOU ALSO NEED TO GET A PO BOX AT YOUR LOCAL POST OFFICE. And you'll need a phone number! Having a separate phone for your business will make it easier for you to deduct it as a legitimate business expense.

Get a Tax ID Number

••• If you are not hiring employees, then you do not need an Employer Identification Number (EIN), and if you are a sole proprietor, then your Social Security Number can be your EIN. However, if you will be hiring employees, you will need to apply for an EIN.

You do not need an EIN if you are a single-member LLC, but if you are or become a multiple-member LLC, then you need to apply for an EIN.

The IRS website has more information about applying for an EIN, including a short set of questions you can answer to determine whether you even need one.

Get a Sales Tax License

If you will be selling products, even if those products are just batting and thread, you will need a Retail Sales Tax License. Check with your state to see how to apply for this. Once you have it, you can use your Sales Tax ID number to set up wholesale accounts with suppliers, which helps prove that you are a legitimate business and saves you money.

••• You will have to file sales tax returns and pay sales tax to the state, either quarterly or yearly, based on the rules in your location, and how much you owe.

Get a Merchant's License

This may also be known as a *business license*, depending on where you are located. When I lived within the city limits of a town, I had a business license with the town, which I obtained at city hall. I now operate outside city limits, and in my county, I need a merchant's license, which I obtain through the county collector's office. Because I don't live within city limits, I no longer need a business license with the city.

IF YOU LIVE WITHIN CITY LIMITS, YOU MAY NEED A BUSINESS LICENSE WITH THE CITY, AND ALSO A MERCHANT'S LICENSE WITH THE COUNTY. Be sure to check with your local city and county government offices to see what type of licenses you need to operate your business in your home, and how and where to obtain them. If you are caught operating a business without the proper licenses, you could be subject to fines or even being shut down.

Set Up a Business Bank Account

Bookkeeping will be a whole lot easier if you keep your business and personal bank accounts separate from the very beginning. If you hire an accountant, they will most likely insist that you have a separate bank account for your business. Besides, it's one more way to prove that you're serious about your business. And did I mention it makes things easier?

IF YOU INTEND TO PURCHASE ITEMS OR SUPPLIES FOR YOUR BUSINESS USING A CREDIT CARD, THEN YOU SHOULD ALSO APPLY FOR A CREDIT CARD FOR YOUR BUSINESS, AND USE IT ONLY FOR BUSINESS PURPOSES, KEEPING IT SEPARATE FROM YOUR PERSONAL CREDIT CARDS. In the event you ever decide to ask for business financing (upgrading your machine, perhaps?), this will help establish a good credit record for your business.

Check Local Requirements

Be sure to ask your lawyer and accountant if they can think of any other forms, licenses, taxes, or regulations you need to be aware of when you start up. Check your state's website for information on starting a business to see if you've forgotten anything important as well. Ask at city hall or the county courthouse to see if you've done everything you need to do to operate legally from your home. Once you've filed all the required forms and done the paperwork, you should be all set!

**HERE'S A HANDY CHECKLIST FOR YOU
TO MAKE SURE YOU'VE COVERED EVERYTHING.**

YES	NO	
_____	_____	Do I need to apply for a zoning variance for it to be legal to operate a business from my home?
_____	_____	If I need a zoning variance, have I applied?
_____	_____	Have I chosen a business entity?
_____	_____	If I'm choosing to become an LLC, have I filed all the necessary forms?
_____	_____	Have I chosen a name for my business?
_____	_____	Have I checked to make sure that name is not already taken?
_____	_____	Have I filed a Fictitious Name Registration, if necessary?
_____	_____	Do I need an EIN?
_____	_____	If yes, have I applied for one?
_____	_____	Have I applied for a Retail Sales Tax license?
_____	_____	Have I applied for my Business / Merchant's License(s)?
_____	_____	Do I have a business bank account set up?
_____	_____	Do I need a business credit card?
_____	_____	If yes, have I applied for one?
_____	_____	Do I have a business phone?
_____	_____	Do I need a post office box?
_____	_____	Is there anything else specific to my location that I need to do?
_____	_____	_____
_____	_____	_____
_____	_____	_____

CRAFT THE PERFECT BUSINESS PLAN

I bet you think I'm gonna tell you that you *have* to have a formal business plan. Well, I'm not!

YOU DON'T *HAVE* TO HAVE A FORMAL BUSINESS PLAN.

Yep, I said it. You don't!

However ... there are three good reasons why I think you *do* need some sort of a business plan:

1. It can help you define your vision for your business.

2. It can help you make decisions easier.

3. It can help you get financial help, if you're asking.

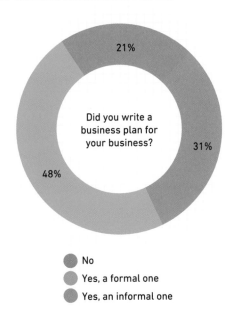

Did you write a business plan for your business?

21%

31%

48%

● No
● Yes, a formal one
● Yes, an informal one

Some say that if you don't have a business plan, then you are not taking your business seriously enough, that you're being unprofessional, or that you're setting yourself up for failure. While I don't think those things are completely true, you can decide for yourself how much of a business plan you need to craft for yourself. As you work through this book, you will come up with a lot of information that will be helpful for your business plan as well.

Business experts all say that you *do* need a business plan, and there are as many ways to craft the perfect business plan as there are to skin a cat (as my grandma would say). There are many resources online that you can use for help with this, as well as books at your local library that you can check out. For more help on this topic, be sure to check this book's Resources (page 205).

THE MAIN REASON YOU WILL NEED A FORMAL BUSINESS PLAN IS IF YOU INTEND TO SEEK FINANCIAL HELP STARTING UP YOUR BUSINESS (SUCH AS FOR THE PURCHASE OF A LONGARM MACHINE). If you do not need financial help with your startup, then a more simplified version of a business plan can help serve as a road map to keep you on track as you get going. Revising it every year will alert you to whether you're doing as you had planned, or if you need to adjust and alter your course.

Have a goal-setting meeting with yourself at the beginning of each year. During this meeting, go over the past year's wins and fails, and plan what you will do for the next year. Include updating your business plan in this meeting, and you'll have plenty of information to keep your business running smoothly.

Even if you don't build a formal business plan, you will need to know this information, and while you may not need to delve quite as deeply into the more nitty-gritty bits, there might be a reason that you *would* need to. So, don't skip this part.

Do the hard work. It'll be worth it.

HERE ARE THE SECTIONS THAT YOUR BUSINESS PLAN SHOULD
INCLUDE. I'LL GO OVER EACH OF THESE THINGS IN TURN.

- Cover Sheet
- Table of Contents
- Introduction
- Mission Statement
- Overview (of the business)
- Economic Analysis
- Financial Analysis
- Market Analysis
- Summary
- Appendix (if necessary)

Cover Sheet

The first thing your business plan will need is a cover sheet or
title page. This page contains the name of your business, your name
as the owner (and, of course, if you have a business partner, that
person's name as well), physical business address, phone number,
website address, and email address.

Table of Contents

While this should be the second page of your plan, you will want to
wait until you have the rest of the plan completed to go back and fill
this in with the proper section names and page numbers.

Introduction

The introduction's purpose is to provide a brief overview of the plan
that follows. You will state your business's general purpose here,
and the key word is "brief." Don't get long-winded in this section,
because you'll be explaining everything in long, boring detail
later on!

Mission Statement

Some experts say that your mission statement can be as long as two pages, but I really believe that keeping this section brief and to the point is much better. Still, it does need to contain three key items:

1. You need to describe what your business does for its customers. What services do you provide? Are you committed to quality workmanship?

2. You need to state your overall business philosophy and the values you will operate by. Do you believe in providing superior customer service? (Of course, you do!) Will you operate with integrity? (Of course, you will!)

3. Remember your "*Why?!*" (page 23) from Chapter 1? You need to put a little bit of that into your mission statement. What is your business's purpose? Describe why you're so passionate about it.

These three things can overlap and run together until you have a few concise sentences that give your business something to operate by in a nutshell. And don't worry if you don't have it perfect the first time. It's *your* mission statement, and you can revise it any time you wish!

NOTES

Overview of the Business

Have you done your research? You should be able to put this section together by referring to the work you do throughout this book. If you work your way through this book, this section will very nearly write itself.

SOME THINGS YOU WILL WANT TO INCLUDE HERE:

- ○ The legal structure you have chosen for your business
- ○ Your business location
- ○ Owner information (you)
- ○ Your qualifications and experience
- ○ The complete nature of your business, and the services you provide
- ○ Your business objectives, both short-term and long-term

Economic Analysis

Because your business can (and probably will) be affected by the health of the quilting industry as a whole, use this section to report on the current state of the economy as it relates to the quilting industry: growth trends, seasonal fluctuations, legal issues, strengths, and weaknesses.

Look online for the most recent survey results to help you with this section. There have been various formats over the years, such as those by Quilting in America and Premier Needle Arts, which periodically report on the state of the industry.

Financial Analysis

This will probably be the most difficult section of your entire business plan to write. If you're just starting up, it's mostly conjecture, and you don't have very much solid information to go on, since you don't know how your business will go yet. If you're already started, it'll be somewhat easier to come up with the numbers. But the main things to keep in mind with this section are (1) to be realistic and (2) to estimate on the conservative side.

I tend to get all pie-in-the-sky and overestimate exactly how much I can get done in a certain period of time, or how much money I'll have coming in, and usually end up disappointed. I also tend to think I'm making at least $20 an hour every day, when in reality, there are days I've worked the entire day for about 50 cents!

Especially if you are seeking financial help to get your business started, this section should contain information that will show what you need to get started, and to project how much you can expect to make, especially in your first year. Ideally, you should project your income and expenses out for the next five years. And don't forget to pay yourself a salary, even if it's meager at first.

INCLUDE AT LEAST THE FOLLOWING INFORMATION:

→ Capital requirements

→ Startup costs

→ How much of your own money you will contribute to your startup

→ Projected income, supported with evidence and statistics

→ A one-year budget, showing your projected expenses

→ A break-even analysis that compares your projected income and expenses to help you estimate profits and determine whether your business will even be viable

A few longarm companies have some useful information on their websites about how to project profits, so if you don't have your own historical data to use, it might help. For a list of longarm companies, see Resources (page 205).

I did interview my own banker to see what she would say if I were to ask them for a loan for a longarm machine. Here are some of the highlights of our conversation:

✳ I would not necessarily have to have a formal business plan, but I would need to have a down payment, and be able to prove that I can make the loan payments on time.

✳ To do that, she said they would prefer that it not all be simply projections—I'd need some real-life data to back it up.

✳ If I don't have enough data, they would want to know if I have other income that they can consider, or if I have any personal property that I could put up as collateral.

✳ It is easier to get financing if you're already established, even as a hobby. Which presents a catch-22: You can't get the machine without being established—you can't get established without the machine.

And keep in mind that my bank is a small-town privately-owned bank, not one of the big "chain" banks, and my banker knows me personally. In fact, she's my cousin! So, you would have to check with your bank to see what kinds of rules they have about lending money to a small startup. They may not be as lenient about loaning money without you having a formal business plan.

Market Analysis

FOR THIS SECTION, YOU WILL NEED TO DO A BIT OF RESEARCH ON
YOUR COMPETITION:

Who are they?

What are they doing (types of quilting they do, extra services they provide)?

What will you be doing that is different?

What is their pricing structure like?

What is their backlog?

What is their turnaround time?

Where do their customers come from?

Will you be able to get customers, too? (Yes, you will!)

50

QUILTING FOR HIRE

Summary

Wrap things up with a few sentences about your business in general. Or if you think you've covered everything and don't have anything more to say, you can leave this out, but think of it as a sort of "In Conclusion" section— remember having to write speeches or essays like that in school?

Appendix

Here is where you will include any supporting documents to further your case. You can include charts, graphs, information about your machine (such as a brochure), articles from industry magazines or websites that will provide further information or back up your previous claims.

2: FIRST STEPS

Remember: Once you've created this document, it's important to update it at least annually. You need to keep an updated road map in front of you, so you know where you're headed!

There! You did it! It's done.

But then again, it's not. Read on. ...

Although it's not normally listed as part of a formal business plan, and even if all you have is an informal business plan, or if you don't have a business plan at all, there is still one thing you need to plan for.

You need to formulate an exit strategy for your business.

Why Is an Exit Strategy Important?

Well, hopefully, you will eventually decide to retire from your business, and you want to have a graceful plan in place for how to handle that.

> ••• But meanwhile, what if something happens that causes you to need to shut down suddenly, before you're ready for that graceful retirement? No one wants to imagine it, but what if a health or family event, or a natural disaster of some sort, suddenly prevents you from continuing to work? What if you're incapacitated, and someone else needs to take care of this for you? You need to have a plan for that. It's important.

Here are some things you'll need to consider:

WHO WILL BE TAKING CARE OF THINGS IF YOU ARE UNABLE TO DO IT YOURSELF?

This could be a spouse, child, family member, or another designated individual that you trust and have discussed this with. It's important to keep this updated, in case the person you've chosen is no longer willing or able to do this for you.

WHO CAN YOU DESIGNATE TO BE YOUR HELPER IN THIS INSTANCE?

HOW WILL CUSTOMERS BE CONTACTED, AND UNFINISHED QUILTS RETURNED TO THEM?

Do you have all the pending quilts in your possession labeled with enough information that your helper will be able to determine who they get returned to and how to do that? Do you have enough insurance to cover the customer quilts in your possession in the event of a natural disaster? I'll talk more about this in Chapter 6.

WHAT WILL BE DONE WITH YOUR SUPPLIES AND EQUIPMENT?

Do you want your machine(s) to be sold or given to someone special? How do you want your supplies and other equipment to be dispersed? Will your helper understand what these items are worth? If your helper is your spouse, do you want them to know?!

WHO WILL TAKE CARE OF THE FINAL PAPERWORK? AND HOW WILL THEY DO THAT?

Have you properly recorded helpful information so your affairs can be easily handled? I have a three-ring binder set up with my information so that my daughter (my current designated helper) will be able to easily handle all the various aspects of shutting down my business, or easily find those who can help her with it.

INCLUDE THINGS SUCH AS:

○ Online account logins and passwords

○ Bank account and credit card information

○ Contact information for people you deal with: accountant, insurance agent, website people, customers, suppliers, ...

○ Instructions for returning unfinished quilts, how to dispense with your equipment and supplies, how to shut down your website or online presence (such as social media accounts), ...

○ Any other instructions you can provide to make this process easier for your helper

**DO YOU HAVE THE MOST IMPORTANT INFORMATION OFF-SITE
SO THAT IN THE EVENT OF A NATURAL DISASTER, IT'S NOT
COMPLETELY GONE?**

You can keep a copy of your information with your helper
or another family member, in a fire- and waterproof box
or safe within your home or in a safe-deposit box at your
bank. You can even put important computer files on a
flash drive and keep it with your other information. If
your information is not stored directly with your helper,
make sure they know where to find it if they need it.

Know that this will require you to keep this information very current
and updated, but if you simply set aside time every few months to
check it over, it's an easy task to do, and will be greatly valuable to
you or your helper, should it (heaven forbid) ever be needed. And if
you're simply ready to retire, it'll help you think of all that needs to
be done to make the process easier.

CREATE AN ACTION PLAN

NOW THAT YOU KNOW WHAT YOU NEED TO DO TO GET YOUR BUSINESS ALL SET UP, IT'S TIME TO IMPLEMENT A PLAN FOR ACTUALLY GETTING IT DONE. It's a lot of work, and some of it will take time—you will need to schedule appointments, have meetings, make phone calls, spend time online or at the library, and do a lot of paperwork. It might be easy to procrastinate on these things because they seem difficult, and you'd rather be quilting, but you really need to do them.

I've found that I work better toward a goal if that goal has a firm deadline. Try to come up with a realistic date that you'd like to be officially open for business. Then set some goals related to getting things done, and establish a timeline for meeting those goals so you can get started running your business and making money quilting for hire!

Sit down with yourself and your calendar, discuss it with your family if you need to, and then plug some of those activities into your days. You may not have to have everything done before you can start, so do the most important tasks first. You can do the rest even after you're up and going.

Use the checklists provided within this chapter to get you started and fill out the lists below so you know what you have to do.

*

FORMS TO FILE:

SCHEDULED DUE DATE:

_____

_____

_____

_____

CALLS/APPOINTMENTS TO MAKE:

_____

_____

_____

_____

BOOKS TO READ:

_____

_____

_____

_____

THINGS TO RESEARCH:

_____

_____

_____

_____

Did this chapter leave you exhausted? I know it was a lot of work! You may still have a lot of work left to do, but at least give yourself credit for getting this far. Maybe a dish of ice cream is in order? Then you can tackle Chapter 3.

CHAPTER 3

hanging out your shingle

NOW THAT YOU HAVE A PLAN, AND ALL YOUR FORMS, LICENSES, AND PAPERWORK ARE IN ORDER, you've got to get ready to open the doors for business. I know you've already been thinking about a lot of these things, but we'll go into a bit more detail to make sure you have everything covered.

LOCATION

Should you work from home or from an off-site studio?

Below are some pros and cons of each from some fellow longarmers. Add your own ideas to this list to help you decide if you will be able to work at home or if an off-site location would be more suitable.

Working from Home

PROS

I can work in my pajamas.

I'm more present for my family, just in case.

My schedule can be a bit more flexible.

No studio rent/lease expense.

Home office deduction on taxes.

No commute.

Close to the fridge.

I won't forget to take anything along to work.

Easy to take breaks.

_____

_____

_____

_____

_____

CONS

I work in my pajamas.

Possibly more interruptions.

Harder to keep work/family balance.

Close to the fridge.

Temptation to do house/family stuff instead of working.

A bit isolated.

_____

_____

_____

_____

_____

_____

_____

Working Off-Site

PROS

Easier to keep work and family separated.

More convenient to meet with clients.

Possibly fewer interruptions from family.

No house distractions
(such as laundry or chores).

CONS

I have to get dressed and leave my house.

A commute.

Studio rent/lease expense.

A more rigid schedule with set hours.

What will I do about lunch?

_____

_____

_____

_____

_____

_____

_____

_____

_____

_____

It's possible that your off-site location is situated on your own property, such as a building separate from your house, which would make some of your pros and cons nonissues. While this would also eliminate the cost of renting or leasing a studio space, there will still be costs incurred to maintain the building and use it as your studio, and you will still need to make sure you have proper insurance coverage (see Insurance, page 134, in Chapter 6).

You will also need to decide, for each of these scenarios, how you will be meeting with your clients. Will you be comfortable enough (and have enough insurance coverage) to allow clients onto your property? Or will you set up a time and place to meet them off-site? You will need to build time into your schedule for pickups and deliveries.

••• If you have an off-site studio, you need to set regular operating hours and then stick to them, so customers aren't surprised (or angry) if they show up during your posted hours and you're not there. This can make your schedule a bit less flexible.

If your off-site location is a space you are renting or leasing, make sure the location is zoned for business, and that the owner has a Certificate of Occupancy, if it's required in your city or state. The Certificate of Occupancy is proof that the building is up to code, and that, if the building was built for a specific purpose and that purpose changes, the powers that be are properly notified. This is important, especially if you will be making alterations to the building.

If you rent your home and wish to start your business in your home, be sure to check with your landlord to make sure it's okay.

WHEN CHOOSING A SPACE TO RENT, KEEP IN MIND THE NATURE OF YOUR WORK. You may think of quilting as a quiet activity, but a longarm machine is not necessarily quiet. Imagine if you rent a space on the second floor of a building, and your machine runs all day, and its noise vibrates down to the occupants on the first floor. This can present a real problem.

My studio is on the second floor of our farmhouse, and when my machine is running, My Cowboy says it sounds like a gravel truck is perpetually driving in and out of our driveway! Just something to keep in mind as you shop for a location for your studio. You don't want any ill will with your business neighbors!

My longarm was in our farmhouse's living room for a couple years until we finished enough remodeling that I could move everything upstairs. My daughter was visiting one day and sitting on the couch with My Cowboy; I was working away at the longarm a few feet away. She eventually looked over at My Cowboy and asked, "How can you stand that noise all day long?" Without any hesitation at all, he calmly replied, "It's the sound of money!"

A few months later, My Cowboy and I were on a road trip and stopped into a little quilt shop that offered longarm services, and the machines were running in the back room while I shopped. As I was checking out, I turned to him and said, "I need to apologize to you. I only just now realized how annoying that noise is if you're not the one actually running the machine!" He just smiled and nodded.

EQUIPMENT

In order to do longarm quilting for customers, you will need a long-arm quilting system. If you already have one, then you're ready to get started. If not, or if you are ready to upgrade from your starter machine now that you're getting serious about having a business, you will need to do your research and find the setup that is right for you.

⟶ **This will not be an easy decision.**

⟶ **There are a *lot* of choices out there.**

⟶ **It's a very expensive piece of equipment, so you want to be sure you're making the right decision.**

⟶ **Keep in mind that the longarm machine itself is only half of the equation—the frame it sits on is also of utmost importance.** And if you want a computerized machine, that adds another important item to your research list.

Here's my best advice: Buy the best machine you can afford. Don't skimp or settle. It's the heart and soul of your business, and it's an investment in your business—an investment that will pay for itself.

HERE'S A LIST OF SOME COMMON FEATURES OF LONGARM QUILTING MACHINES AND THEIR FRAMES TO HELP GET YOU STARTED. Put each of these features on the appropriate list that fits your situation. For instance, you may feel a computerized machine is a definite "Yes," but for me it's a "No" feature. Your list will not look exactly like anyone else's list.

Machine Features to Research

Throat size

Variety of stitch lengths

Needle up/down

One-stitch button

Handles

Stitch regulator

Stitch counter

Touch-screen control

Lighting

Computerized or not

If computerized, number of designs offered

Classes/training available

Support available

Ergonomics

Warranty information

Price

Frame Features to Research

Size of frame

Material it is made from (wood, steel, ...)

How smooth is the carriage?

Size of the ratchet increments on the poles

Type of wheels on the carriage

Channel locks

Liftable top roller

Adjustable height

Motorized fabric advance

Steel roller bars (at least 1¾″ in diameter)

Ease of loading a quilt

Ergonomics

Warranty information

Price

In Resources (page 205), you'll find a list of companies that make longarm quilting systems. I recommend that you visit their websites to see what they have to offer and speak with a dealer or a sales rep to ask questions you may have. As you study each type of machine, the frame it sits on, and the options offered with each one, fill out the following three lists.

"YES" LIST	**"MAYBE" LIST**	**"NO" LIST**
features that you *must have*:	features that would be *nice to have*:	features that you *don't really need*:
_____	_____	_____
_____	_____	_____
_____	_____	_____
_____	_____	_____
_____	_____	_____
_____	_____	_____
_____	_____	_____
_____	_____	_____

On the next page is a Longarm Machine Research Checklist that you can fill out for each machine you are considering. Fill in the items from your "Yes" List on that form, and as you study each system, make sure it has all the features from your "Yes" List. Fill in all the blanks and add your own questions to it and make sure you get them answered. Use your list of desired features to help you narrow down your selection.

There is a downloadable version of the Longarm Machine Research Checklist available (see Downloads, page 10)—so you can print it out as many times as you need to.

LONGARM MACHINE RESEARCH CHECKLIST

Name of manufacturer/brand of machine:_____

Model name: _____ Price for complete system: _____

Machine throat space size: _____

Does it have the features that you must have? *(List your must-have features below.)*

_____ ⭘ YES ⭘ NO   _____ ⭘ YES ⭘ NO

_____ ⭘ YES ⭘ NO   _____ ⭘ YES ⭘ NO

_____ ⭘ YES ⭘ NO   _____ ⭘ YES ⭘ NO

_____ ⭘ YES ⭘ NO   _____ ⭘ YES ⭘ NO

Other features of this system (extras that are simply nice to have):

_____   _____

_____   _____

Write down any other questions you want to ask about this model. Consider such things as maintenance, technical support, training, and so on.

_____

_____

_____

What size is the frame? _____ How much floor space will it require? _____

Are the rollers made of quality steel, and at least 1¾″ in diameter?
⭘ YES ⭘ NO

Write down any other questions you want to ask about the frame. Make note of any special features of the frame.

_____

_____

_____

If you want a computerized machine, write down all the questions you want to ask about that. Think of such things as ease of use, available support, updates, the library of designs, training, and so on.

_____

_____

_____

Decide What Size Frame You Need

This will determine the maximum quilt size you can take in, so you need to know what that is for your customers. You also need to know if you have the space for it in your home or studio. Plus, you will need to have a plan for getting the frame into your space. The roller bars can be as long as 14 feet, and they don't bend, so make sure you can get them into the space you've chosen. My studio is upstairs in our old farmhouse, but luckily, our staircase is open clear to the top, so we didn't have a problem. Take into consideration tight corners, staircases, and doorways when determining how you will get your machine moved into your space.

And don't forget: The machine is not the only thing you need to have space for. You need to take into account the area around the machine. You need 2 to 3 feet of working space on the front and back of your machine, and you need to be able to get around the frame on at least one end. You will also most likely have other items to store in your longarm area, so keep in mind what furniture pieces you will have and where you will be storing all the other tools and supplies you need at hand. (See Setting Up Your Space, page 104, in Chapter 5.)

Decide What Size Machine You Need

I'm mostly referring to the size of the throat space here, which is the distance from the needle to the back upright portion of the machine.

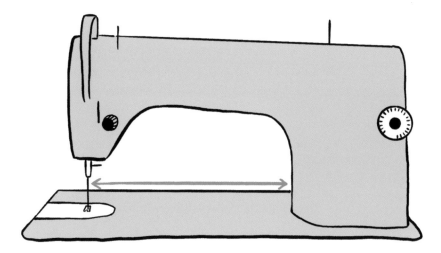

BIG THROAT SPACE

❋ You can quilt a larger area before having to advance the quilt on the frame.

❋ It's a lot further to reach across the quilt, so if you're shorter, this could be a problem.

❋ It's good for computerized machines, since they can cover more area and do a greater variety of designs.

SMALL THROAT SPACE

❋ You will spend more time advancing the quilt on the frame.

❋ It may limit the patterns you can do.

❋ It reduces the area you have to work in.

❋ It can seriously hinder your productivity.

I personally recommend buying **A MACHINE WITH A MEDIUM-SIZED THROAT SPACE OF 20 TO 26 INCHES.** But I encourage you to do your own extensive research and pick the machine that is best for you.

In addition to the frame and the machine itself, don't forget to **CONSIDER THE LIGHTING** you will need to be able to work comfortably. Some companies sell a lighting system along with the machine, but there are also third-party options you might like better—or you could simply have them built into your studio, which is what I have. Do your research.

And… definitely consider some **CUSHIONED FLOOR MATS** to lay on the floor where you'll be standing—your body will thank you for it!

Some longarm quilters use **A SADDLE STOOL OR A ROLLING CHAIR**, which allows them to sit while running their machine. If this seems like something you might need, look into the options available.

Talk to a Representative

BE SURE TO TALK TO A REPRESENTATIVE FOR EACH LONGARM BRAND you're considering, and ask them all the questions you can possibly think of asking. Keep your form handy during your discussion, so you can ask them about all the various features. You will know what questions you want to ask, and you can jot down notes from your discussion, as well as price quotes.

Test-Drive at Quilt Shows

AT LARGE QUILT SHOWS, ALL THE MAJOR LONGARM MANUFACTURERS USUALLY HAVE A BOOTH SET UP with a lot of their machine models on the floor ready for you to test-drive. Take full advantage of this. Have your forms all filled out and ready to go. Take them along with you and get the answers to all your questions. Do this for every model you are considering, so you can make your own comparisons and narrow down your decision.

Attend Open Houses at Dealers

IF THERE IS A DEALER NEARBY FOR A BRAND YOU ARE CONSIDERING, ATTEND ANY OPEN HOUSE–type events they might have so you can take a test-drive and ask questions. If they have a showroom that you can visit anytime, simply drop in and shop around.

Ask Fellow Longarmers

FIND OUT WHAT TYPE OF MACHINE THEY HAVE AND ASK THEM WHY THEY CHOSE IT. Would they choose it again? What are their likes and dislikes about it? Their favorite features? Are they able to get the support they need?

••• Once you've tried several different brands of machines, talked to reps from each company, compared the features of each, and gotten all your questions answered, it's time to narrow down your selection.

Keep testing, asking questions, studying the forms you've filled out, and comparing features until you have it so fine-tuned that your final selection becomes obvious. At that point, you're ready to find a dealer and make your purchase! Scary, huh? The day I bought my machine, I called My Cowboy to tell him I had done it and was so sick to my stomach, I thought I was gonna pass out!

AFTER YOU'VE MADE YOUR SELECTION, PURCHASED YOUR SYSTEM, AND GOTTEN IT DELIVERED AND ALL SET UP, IT'S TIME TO PRACTICE, PRACTICE, PRACTICE. You can't begin quilting for others until you are comfortable with the system and can do presentable work. The learning curve may be bigger than you first believed. I remember thinking, a few days in, "What have I done?" But don't give up. Keep at it. Watch videos, take classes, ask other quilters, and keep practicing. Before long, you'll be a pro!

In selecting my longarm, I dabbled for over a year, test-driving at shows, reading up on machines, talking to people who had machines, and comparing features. When I started seriously shopping, I tried six different models. At the AQS Show in Paducah, Kentucky, in the spring of 2009, I narrowed it down to my top three, and spent a lot of time talking to the representatives in each booth about the machines I was considering. In the end, it came down to three things: weight of the machine and how it rode its frame, the noise level of the machine, and the support I would be able to get.

I settled on an older refurbished Nolting 24″ machine. Ten months later I traded "Florence" in for another step up, and I've had the same machine ever since. "Ivy" is a 2004 Nolting 24″ Pro model (noncomputerized), and we get along so well that even though I've considered trading her in for a newer model, I simply can't do it because she works so well for me. She's low maintenance, and a real workhorse. We make a great team.

TOOLS AND SUPPLIES

In addition to the longarm quilting system, you will want and need various tools and supplies to use with it. Some of these things you will need right away, like a bobbin winder and oil. Other things, such as a ruler plate, can possibly wait. It's a good idea to use your machine for a while so that you will know whether you even need some of the gadgets you're contemplating. You can decide which are most important to you, and set up a budget to help you acquire them over time.

HERE ARE A FEW TOOLS AND SUPPLIES TO CONSIDER:

Bobbins	Needles	Scissors
Bobbin winder	Pantograph patterns (paper or digital)	Spare light bulbs
Machine oil		Batting
Marking utensils	Ruler plate	Thread
Measuring instruments	Rulers	

 With all these things, you can start small and add to your inventory as your budget allows.

For a list of suppliers, see Resources (page 205). In the case of batting and thread suppliers, contact them to see if you can set up a wholesale account, and find out what their terms are. This is where that Retail Sales Tax number comes in handy!

THINGS TO CONSIDER

o You will constantly be seeing new tools come on the market that you may want. Factor this into your budget so that you can periodically purchase some new things for your business.

o It takes time to build up a solid inventory of thread so that you always have just the right color on hand for any quilt that comes in.

o It also takes a while to collect enough pantograph patterns, so you feel you have a good selection to offer to your customers who want that type of quilting (both the paper type and the digital type).

o If you plan to keep batting on hand to sell to your customers, you will need to decide what types are the best to keep in stock, and purchase enough to have a good selection for them to choose from.

o If you plan to carry a selection of quilt backing fabrics for your clients to choose from and purchase from you, you will need to find a supplier and have some on hand.

BUILD YOUR BRAND

"A brand is more than just a logo." ~ **AUTHOR**

YOUR BRAND SHOULD REFLECT THE PERSONALITY OF YOUR BUSINESS. You want it to set you apart from your competition and represent you well. You want it to leave a favorable impression on your customers, and be something people will come to recognize over time. You want it to fit the vibe of your business and be easy to recognize and understand.

Your brand represents the look and feel of your business, and includes such things as your logo, the typefaces and colors you use, your marketing materials, the way you write your blog posts, how you appear in videos, and your social media presence.

Every interaction with your clients is part of their experience with your brand, and you want that experience to be memorable—in a good way!

You don't *have* to have a brand, but by having one, you signal to your audience that you are taking your business seriously and have put some thought into what you're doing. Fortunately, building a brand for a service-based business is not as difficult (or expensive) as building a brand for a product-based business.

You don't have to spend a lot of money on this all at once. Don't let this keep you from starting. You can let it evolve over time, because brand recognition doesn't happen overnight anyway. Perhaps get a logo first so that you can have business cards printed, and add in the other things along the way, as they seem necessary or important.

HOW DO YOU WANT YOUR BUSINESS TO BE SEEN?

It can be a combination of several of these things.

Classic

Fun

Traditional

Serious

Handmade

Elegant

Modern

Funky

Minimalistic

Fancy

Playful

Rustic

Are there certain colors you'd like to use? Using only one or two colors is best.

_____

_____

Any particular style of typeface that you feel would be right for your business? Make sure it's something that is easily legible. You also want it to fit the style of your business. For example, if you do mostly modern quilting, you will want your brand to have a modern look and feel.

_____

_____

Once you've decided on a certain look or vibe you'd like your business to have, you will need to design a logo.

If you are able to do this yourself, or if you have a friend or family member who can do this for you free of charge, great! Go for it. It will save you money. Once you've come up with your idea, run it past your family or some close friends to get some feedback. See if they think it represents you well and that it is easy to read and identify.

If you don't want to do this yourself, hire it out. Your designer will meet with you to discuss the look and feel you're trying to convey, and then present you with several designs to choose from based on what you've discussed. In your initial meeting, be prepared with information on possible typefaces and colors you'd like to use, and what sort of look you're going for. They often charge by the hour, so make the most of your time by being well prepared.

MAKE SURE YOUR LOGO IS LEGIBLE AT SEVERAL DISTANCES AND IN VARIOUS SIZES. Maybe you can read it just fine close up, but when you back off, does it still make sense, or is it just a jumble of colors and letters that blends into a background? Maybe it looks great on your website, but when reduced down to fit on a business card, it looks awful. Audition it carefully and choose your colors wisely. If you are using colors, make sure that your logo still looks good in only one color, such as all black, or all white, in instances where it might need to be used like that.

Once you have your logo, you can use it on your website, business cards, stationery, invoices, brochures, products, and marketing materials, creating a consistent look for everything to do with your business. It will also become an important part of the design of your entire website, where you can use the same colors and typefaces to create a cohesive look for your online presence.

ESTABLISH YOUR ONLINE PRESENCE

There are several ways you can establish an online presence. Some are more expensive than others. You can build this up slowly over time, and decide how important it is to your business, then decide what level you will build it to.

HERE ARE SEVERAL OPTIONS.

Use Social Media

Some quilters have built successful businesses using only Facebook or Instagram.

As soon as you have named your business and filed your fictitious name registration, you should set up, at a minimum, the accounts listed below, simply to make sure that no one else on those platforms has the same name as you. This will ensure that someone else doesn't beat you to the punch and use the name you were planning to use on that platform. Even if you don't start using all of them right away, at least you will have your business's name reserved for when you're ready.

- ⬤ Set up a business page on Facebook.
- ⬤ Set up a business account on Instagram.
- ⬤ Set up an account on Twitter.
- ⬤ Start a business Pinterest page to display your work.

I'll talk more about using these to your advantage in Chapter 7.

Start Writing a Blog

A few free blog hosting sites are available, and they are fairly easy to set up and start using right away. You can use one of the free blogging sites if you simply want to write a blog, but if you are also planning to get a website, it's best to have your blog incorporated into that from the start, so plan ahead if this is what you want.

Some people say that blogging is dying, but I don't believe that's true. Blogs are a great way to impart more detailed information to your followers than you can include in a Facebook or Instagram post. IF YOUR BLOG IS PART OF YOUR WEBSITE, IT CAN LEAD READERS TO EXPLORE OTHER PARTS OF YOUR WEBSITE MORE EASILY AND POTENTIALLY ENTICE THEM TO BECOME ONE OF YOUR CUSTOMERS. You can use social media to direct people to your blog for more information.

And here's the thing: Your blog is yours. It's not controlled by an arbitrary algorithm. Your readers can subscribe to your blog, which means they get emails with information directly from you that they voluntarily signed up for and want to have. This gives you a way to let them know things you want them to know without having to take a chance on whether an algorithm has alerted them to your new post or not.

Consider a monthly or quarterly email newsletter that imparts information specifically for your subscribers. Reward them for being subscribers with special information or discount codes and specials only for subscribers. And then tell *all* your readers about it, so that if they want to get this special information, too, they should subscribe! Make it easy for them to subscribe by having a simple form to fill out right on your blog's main page. If you need help with this, ask your web folks to help you set it up (continue to Get a Website, next page). They can also provide training for you on how to do successful email campaigns.

Get a Website

A website—one with your own domain name that represents your business—can do so many things to help your business be successful. Think about it: When you first hear of something or someone new, it's almost second nature to try to find them online. If someone types in your name or the name of your business, wouldn't it be great if your website popped up for them to explore?

A good website does cost money, with expenses like buying a domain name, hosting the site, keeping it updated and compliant, doing updates, keeping all the information current, and so on. But if you want to grow your business, it is well worth it.

If you want a professional website, it's a good idea to hire someone to build it for you. If it's not in your budget to do this right away, I would still suggest that you go ahead and purchase your domain name as soon as possible, just to make sure that no one else gets it before you do. You can talk to someone who does website design and hosting for help with how to do this.

Your website designer (even if you're using a friend or relative for this) is going to want to know how you want your site to look. Since you have your brand all hashed out, you should be able to give them really good information on the style, fonts, colors, and the general look and feel you're after.

BUT THERE'S A LOT MORE TO IT. • ▶

* You need to decide what information you'll be putting on your site and how it will be organized.

* You will need clear, informative copy for each section, plus photos.

* You want your website to be easy to navigate, so your visitors have a good experience. Think of some websites you admire, and make note of the features that make you like them so much.

* You should have an About page that gives visitors a bit of personal information about you and your business.

* You need a way for visitors to easily contact you.

* You may want a page that shows thumbnail images of all the different pantographs you have to offer your customers.

* You may need a Gallery page to show your work.

* Your blog should be part of your main site.

* You need to provide links to all your social media accounts.

With so much to consider, hiring website professionals to do all this for you is money well spent. Your web folks can help you with all the necessary plug-ins, help you stay compliant with all the current internet rules and requirements, and do backups and updates for you. They can also help you analyze how well your site is working and show you all sorts of data related to your site. They can also suggest ways to improve your visitors' experience on your site and grow your following (you can even pay them to do that for you!).

AND REMEMBER, IT DOESN'T ALL HAVE TO BE DONE AT ONCE. Build it into your budget and do additions and upgrades as you can afford them. My web people do a free site review with me annually and then present me with a list of things I could do to improve my site. I get to pick and choose the things I want from the list, and then I request them to be done as I can afford them.

CHAPTER 4

setting customer expectations

NOW THAT YOU'RE OPEN FOR BUSINESS, CUSTOMERS WILL START TO FIND YOU. You will need to know who your ideal clients are, and what you can do for them. Not everyone who comes knocking will be a good fit for your services, so this chapter is going to help you decide exactly what you will offer so you can be confident in accepting or declining the jobs that come your way.

WHAT SERVICES WILL YOU PROVIDE?

QUILTING FOR SOMEONE ELSE CAN CAUSE A LOT OF STRESS! You have a responsibility to your customers to take their carefully stitched creations and put the finishing touch on them. Even if you've been quilting for months (or even years) for yourself—practicing and building up to this moment—going into business for real can be scary. You should think carefully about what services you feel comfortable providing.

→ You may only feel comfortable doing computerized quilting, to minimize the possibility of messing up.

→ You may only feel comfortable stitching out a few tried-and-true designs that you are familiar with and can do easily. If so, you can offer a limited selection of pattern choices to your customers.

→ You may have come to the point where you have built up enough experience to do custom quilting and enjoy working with your clients to come up with the perfect plan to add that final layer of design to their quilt tops.

→ You may even be beyond that and be able to do highly custom, heirloom-type quilting for a chosen few.

→ You may be willing to do all of the above.

→ You may start out at one level and graduate through all of them.

→ You may work your way up and then decide to work your way back down!

Will you offer other services as well?

OTHER SERVICES CAN INCLUDE:

* **Piecing and preparing quilt backing**

* **Selling batting and backing**

* **Trimming**

* **Binding (including specialty binding)**

* **Basting a quilt for hand quilting**

* **Making/attaching hanging sleeves**

* **Making/attaching labels**

Decide if any of these other services are things you feel comfortable with and are skilled enough to provide and include them in your offerings.

... It's wise to know what your competition is up to, but ultimately, don't base your business plans on what they're doing. You don't have to follow the crowd. What do you do that is different from your competition? What makes you unique? What can you do to set yourself apart? That may help you decide which services you'd like to concentrate on the most.

And once you do know what your competition is up to, don't worry about it. Don't fear your competition, because there's room for everyone. Just "tend to yer own knittin'," as my grandma would say, and do your own best work.

FIND YOUR CUSTOMERS

Now that you know what services you will be providing, you need to know who you will be willing to provide these services for!

 The day I bought my machine, my sales rep said to me, "If you are going into business, do not quilt for friends and family for free." And he left it at that. I'll leave you to figure out why that's good advice.

If you are just starting out, you will probably have time in your schedule to accept any job that comes your way. This will teach you a *lot* about what types of quilting you enjoy, which jobs are the most profitable and enjoyable, and even which customers you don't want to work with a second time!

••• If someone asks you to do something you're not comfortable with and you don't think you have the skills to do it justice, don't feel bad referring them to someone else. I keep a list of other quilters in my area who do things I don't do, and I pass out their information quite regularly. It's better to be honest and lose the job, than to accept the job and screw it up. Your reputation is at stake, and word of mouth is a strong form of advertising, both good and bad.

As you gain experience and become a better quilter from all the practice, you may want to offer even more custom quilting, and you will want to have an idea of exactly what type of clients you would like to attract.

If you want to do a certain type of quilting, yet no one is hiring you for that type of work, do some projects of your own in that style of quilting and show them off. You can show your work at guild meetings, in quilt shows, on your blog and website, and on all your social media channels. Word will get around and you will eventually attract your dream client.

BUT YOU NEED TO KNOW:

⟶ Who is my dream client?

⟶ What types of quilts will my dream clients be asking me to work on?

⟶ Do I want to have tight deadlines? Or work at my own pace?

⟶ Can I handle the pressure of highly custom quilting? And tight deadlines?

⟶ Or would I rather only do pantographs?

YOUR DREAM CLIENT MAY BE ...

... a meticulous quilter who creates fantastically intricate quilt tops and wants you to add a layer of custom quilting that sets off their hard work in an excellent way, so you work together to come up with the perfect quilting plan.

... a quilter who does fast and easy quilts, wants a quick turnaround with a simple pantograph, and brings you several quilts a month.

... a quilter who does fabulous appliqué and wants your skills to enhance their fine needlework, while not overpowering the effect they've already created.

... someone who always wants a computerized design or a pantograph.

... someone who makes utility quilts and simply wants you to do enough to hold them together so they hold up to a lot of use and loving.

... someone who brings you their quilt top and says, "Do whatever you want to it."

... an art quilter who wants you to perform your own layer of thread-painted art on top of what they've created.

... a collector of vintage quilt tops who wants them finished by machine, while still keeping the look and feel of the time period in which they were originally created.

BASED ON THE TYPES OF QUILTING SERVICES YOU OFFER, WHO IS YOUR DREAM CLIENT?

_____

_____

_____

Am I at that level of service? _____

If not, what do I need to do _____
to get to that level?

Do I want to get _____
to that level?

Is their request out of the _____
scope of my offerings?

Am I more comfortable _____
doing just one type
of quilting?

Once you've determined who your dream client is, pay attention to those who do the kind of work you'd like to add your finishing touches to, and reach out to them. Before long, you will have a long list of dream clients and a backlog resembling that of any seasoned professional quilter!

I have a dream client … You may have heard of her: Victoria Findlay Wolfe (page 6). We met through our blogs in 2009, and we've been best friends ever since. I'd only had my longarm for about five months at that time, and I'd only been quilting for customers for about three months. But she sent me some tops to quilt anyway, and I quilted them and sent them back. I can't even remember most of those early quilts (and I shudder to think what type of job I did on them!), but here's the great thing about my dream client: Victoria has constantly pushed me to do and try things I might never have tried otherwise, and I have become a much better quilter because of it. Together we meet tight deadlines, do some intense work, and create some beautiful quilts! Victoria keeps me very busy, so I fill in the gaps with other types of easier quilting, just to give my nerves a break! And because Victoria's work is high-profile, it has brought a lot of new customers my way.

PAPERWORK

My grandmother used to have a sign hanging in her bathroom that said, "No job is finished until the paperwork is done!" *Tee-hee!*

But really, it's true. You can't get paid until the paperwork is done!

There are basically only two forms you will need to complete a customer quilting job. I'll provide some samples of each one that may give you some ideas for how you might want to set yours up.

Take-In Forms

You'll need a take-in form. It might also be known as an *intake form*. Whichever you call it, before we go over what a take-in form includes, here's the reality:

My customers do not fill out their own take-in forms. They usually hand me a bag in a parking lot somewhere or at a guild meeting, and I fill out the take-in form once I get home with the quilt and look it over. Or a quilt will arrive in the mail, and I will start filling out the form when I open the box.

••• In fact, my customers never even see my take-in forms. They are strictly for my own information. I do it for myself to make sure that I have all the information necessary to complete the job. If there are any blanks I can't fill in based on things we've already discussed (either in person or by email), then I can call or email the client to get those questions answered long before it's time to actually load their quilt on the frame.

You might use them minimally after a while. Becky Collis, of Collis Country Quilting, says she rarely uses her form now, because most of her work arrives by mail, and she keeps texts and emails from her clients that contain the information she needs to know.

However, these forms are helpful, especially when you're first starting your business. You may think of your take-in form as more of a document for yourself rather than the client, or maybe you have the client fill it out and then go over it with them. Either way, it doesn't have to be fancy—but there are some basic elements it needs to include:

CUSTOMER CONTACT INFORMATION: **Name, address, phone number, email**

DATES: **Date you took it in, date they need it back**

QUILT INFORMATION: **Quilt name or description, quilt measurements**

QUILTING INFORMATION: **How it is to be quilted (name of pantograph, or style of design), price range to keep it within, thread type and color(s) to use, batting type (and who supplies it), backing information, any extra services you are to provide and the details about them**

PERMISSION: **To post photos online, either on your website or social media accounts**

IF YOU ACCEPT QUILTS BY MAIL, YOU MAY WANT TO INCLUDE A TAKE-IN FORM ON YOUR WEBSITE, WHICH CAN PROVIDE YOU WITH A LOT OF PRELIMINARY INFORMATION. A fine example of an online take-in form is the one used by Ida Larsen, of Ida's Custom Quilts (see Resources, page 205).

I seriously doubt that you need a formal contract for a longarm quilting job. In my experience, that seems like overkill. The take-in form should be enough, but it is an important reference document. If you require an up-front deposit for specific work, such as a highly custom job, then build that into your take-in form for custom work, even if you need to have a second take-in form for that type of quilting.

••• I usually offer first-time customers the opportunity to receive a written quote, if they wish to have one. The information on the take-in form can be used to figure out the amount for the quote. But if you have not seen the quilt for yourself, be sure to make the client aware that, if the quilt differs from what they describe and will cause you more work than you first believed, the quote is subject to change and the final price may be higher.

That being said, most of my clients simply ask for a ballpark estimate after choosing the style of quilting they'd like to have, so I keep the quilting within the price range they've asked for, and we rarely have any bad surprises.

On the next page is a Sample Take-In Form for you to use as a starting point for developing your own.

There is a downloadable version of the Sample Take-In Form available (see Downloads, page 10)—so you can print it out as many times as you need to.

✳ YOUR BUSINESS NAME OR LOGO HERE ✳

- - - - - - - - - - - - - - CUSTOMER INFORMATION - - - - - - - - - - - - - -

Name _____

Street address _____

City _____ State _____ Zip _____

Email _____

Phone _____ Date taken in _____

Date to be completed by _____

- -

Quilt description or name _____

_____

Quilt top size _____ wide × _____ long

Type of quilting and price range desired _____

_____

THREAD

Color/type _____

BATTING

◯ Provided by customer ◯ Provided by me Size _____

Type of batting _____

BACKING

◯ Provided by customer ◯ Provided by me Size _____

If provided by a customer, is prep work done? _____ Or needed? _____

If provided by me, what type? _____

ANY ADDITIONAL SERVICES DESIRED

◯ Trimming ◯ Pressing ◯ Binding ◯ Hanging sleeve

Permission to post photos on blog and social media: ◯ YES ◯ NO

Any special instructions or notes_____

_____

_____

Invoices

Some of your customers won't care to have a copy of the invoice for their quilts. They don't want any evidence lying around! But if your customers are designers or other people who have their own businesses, they will for sure need an invoice for their records. And if you do a lot of long-distance quilting, you will need an invoice to email to your clients or to send back with their finished quilts so you can get paid.

IT'S NICE TO CREATE A PROFESSIONAL-LOOKING INVOICE TO GIVE TO YOUR CUSTOMERS. Most word-processing programs (such as Microsoft Word or Apple Pages) have invoice templates already set up. Some have a spot for you to drop in your logo, and you can customize the fields to include the information you need to provide on your invoice.

••• I try to itemize my invoices, so if a customer ever asks me to "do it just like you did that other one," I can refer back to my invoice and notes to find out the needed information, such as which pantograph I used, what thread color, or what type of batting.

There is a downloadable version of the Sample Invoice available (see Downloads, page 10)—so you can print it out as many times as you need to.

SAMPLE INVOICE

 YOUR BUSINESS NAME OR LOGO HERE

Your street address
Your city, state, zip code
Your phone
Your email

- - - - - - - - - - - - **CUSTOMER INFORMATION** - - - - - - - - - -

Name _____

Street address _____

City _____ State _____ Zip _____

Phone _____ Email _____

- -

DESCRIPTION	PRICE	TOTAL

Thanks for letting me quilt for you!

REACHING AGREEMENT

For those clients who want a pantograph or a computerized design, you need to have a way for them to know what designs they can choose from (either what you have available or what you can acquire).

ONE QUILTER IN MY AREA HAS A LARGE THREE-RING BINDER WITH PICTURES OF HER AVAILABLE DESIGNS FOR HER LOCAL CLIENTS TO THUMB THROUGH. Quilters with websites often put their selections on a website page that you can shop through. I usually send my clients to one of the websites that I purchase my paper pantographs from, so they can shop for themselves. If they choose one I don't already own, I'm willing to buy the one they want and add it to my collection (this would work for digital designs as well). (For some places I recommend, see Resources, page 205.)

For custom quilting, there may need to be a lot of back-and-forth discussion on exactly what designs the client wants included on their quilt, so you need to make a lot of notes based on your discussions so that you know what to do once the quilt is loaded on your machine. Save any email correspondence so that you can refer back to it. I created an email folder specifically to hold emails from my longarm customers. You could even sort that folder by each individual client, if necessary.

Remember, you can't take a customer's quilt and do what *you* want to it. You are in business to give your customers what *they* want. Don't forget this.

Make sure to get some information on the customer's quilting design likes and dislikes as a starting point. Some people like feathers, some don't. Some like heavy background fills, some don't. Do they want modern or traditional quilting?

Be sure that the designs you're discussing are within the client's price range. If they're expecting a custom job for the price of a simple allover, you'll have to compromise on a design they like and will pay for that you can still make money doing. (See Setting Prices, page 123, in Chapter 6.)

••• Remember, your client is bringing their quilt to you
  because they can't or don't want to quilt it themselves,
  and you have made a huge investment in your business.
  You will occasionally have to tactfully educate clients
  who are arguing about price points.

For custom jobs, I like to have a photograph of the quilt ahead of time, so I can think about quilting possibilities. Sometimes I print several copies of the photo and draw all over them with the client's ideas and my ideas for various quilting designs. When we've reached consensus and the quilt arrives, this photo sheet goes with the take-in form so that everything is together and I know what to do.

You can also ask the customer, if they're willing, to draw some ideas on a photo of the quilt to give you some more ideas of what they want. Trust me, this is such a time saver.

Knowing how you will quilt the top before you ever load it on the frame eliminates a lot of what I call the "Stand and Stare Factor."

Disagreements

WHAT HAPPENS IF YOU DON'T AGREE? There comes a time when every quilter has that "trouble customer." Someone who is not happy with the work you've done and maybe even thinks you've ruined their quilt.

"There's no whining in quilting!" ~ **MY COWBOY**

HAVING CAREFUL NOTES ON YOUR TAKE-IN FORM IS ONE WAY TO PROVE THAT YOU DID THE WORK YOU WERE HIRED TO DO, BUT IF THEY'RE SIMPLY UNHAPPY WITH THE WAY IT WAS DONE, YOU NEED TO HAVE A PLAN FOR WHAT YOU WILL DO TO APPEASE THEM.

→ You can offer a partial refund.

→ You can offer to do it (or parts of it) over again.

→ You can bite your tongue, take a hit, and not charge for the job at all.

If a disagreement occurs and you feel you were in the right, try to shrug it off and remember all the good things others say about your work. Handling the incident in a professional manner, keeping your cool, and being the better person will speak volumes.

If you were the one in the wrong, be sincere in your offers to make it right for your client, and do your best to make it right. Good customer service will go a long way toward salvaging your reputation.

SOME CUSTOMERS WILL NEVER BE HAPPY WITH ANYTHING YOU DO. Some are even hoping that by throwing a fit over what they perceive as unacceptable work (even if that is not the case), they will get their quilting job for free. Customers like this can be a huge hit to your confidence, especially if they start badmouthing your work to their friends.

If you ever work for a customer like this, you will know not to accept jobs from them in the future. You can simply tell them that you are not a good fit for them as a quilter, and they need to find someone else to work with.

> "I once had a very wise man for a boss—the best boss I ever had—and he used to always say: 'If they anger you, they conquer you.' Try to keep this in mind if you ever have to deal with a trouble customer." ~ AUTHOR

4: SETTING CUSTOMER EXPECTATIONS

Trouble Quilts

What about quilts that are poorly pieced or have wavy borders, gapping seams, no matching points, or other issues that make it difficult to quilt them?

••• You need to have a policy about how you will handle these situations. Will you flat out turn them down? Charge for fixes/repairs? Do your best to make them look good and explain to the customer the issues you had?

What do you say to the client who hands you a poorly put-together quilt top that they're super-proud of, and says, "Make it show-worthy!"?

What if they bring you a quilt top covered in pet hair or reeking of cigarette smoke? Or an intricately pieced showstopper and ask you to put an allover design on it?

If you don't feel that you can work with the quilt (or its owner) to make the quilt look the way they want it to, then it's okay to turn down the job. If you can't do the quilt any favors with your quilting efforts, then it might be best to turn the job down and save your reputation. Imagine the client showing the quilt and telling people that you were the quilter! Does the quilt top represent you the way you want to be represented? If not, turn it down—tactfully, of course.

If you want to tackle it, discuss any fixes or repairs with the client beforehand. It may be that they are willing to fix the issues themselves but are simply not aware of what those issues are. Or they may be okay with paying you to do it.

••• If you think they are choosing the wrong quilting design for their quilt, kindly and tactfully discuss some better options, but ultimately go with what the customer wants. It may be all they are willing to pay for, and remember, it's not *your* quilt.

But it *is* your reputation—so if you decide not to do it, that's okay. Guard your reputation carefully, so that you can always be proud of your work.

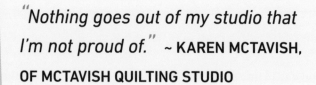

"Nothing goes out of my studio that I'm not proud of." ~ KAREN MCTAVISH, OF MCTAVISH QUILTING STUDIO

SHIPPING AND HANDLING

A GOOD NUMBER OF YOUR CUSTOMERS MAY NOT BE LOCAL TO YOU.
Probably 90% of the quilts I quilt come and go through the mail to
customers who are mostly out of my state.

You need to have a supply of good, sturdy boxes in several sizes;
some packing material, such as air pillows or clean paper to crumple
up (*not* packing peanuts); and a lot of packing tape. A postal scale
that weighs up to 50-pound boxes also comes in handy (you can find
one at your local office-supply store or online). Keep in mind you will
need storage space for these supplies, too.

My Cowboy and I have often made fun of Victoria—her
packages arrive bulging, with shipping tape coating every
square inch of the box! We jokingly call her "The Packing
Tape Queen" here at the ol' ranch.

One day as I was struggling to pack up a quilt to be shipped,
My Cowboy was watching me, and finally asked: "You tryin' to
pull a Victoria? Crammin' 20 pounds of stuff into a 10-pound
box?" I laughed hysterically, gave up, and went to look for a
larger box!

You will need to know what mail services are available in your area
and how to go about utilizing them. Does your USPS mail carrier pick
up packages at your house? What time of day? And how often? Can
you schedule UPS and FedEx pickups from your house? Or do you
have to take them to a drop-off point? If they are not prepaid, is there
a location that can take your payments and generate labels for you?

You can do a lot of your shipping preparation online and usually at a discounted price. For some websites that allow you to order shipping supplies, generate shipping labels, schedule pickups, and track packages, check Resources (page 205).

BE SURE TO GET A TRACKING NUMBER FOR EVERY PACKAGE YOU SEND. Supply this tracking number to your client so they can keep an eye on when it might arrive back to them. I keep an eye on the tracking information and then check with the client to make sure they received it once it says it's been delivered.

If you know that a client is shipping you a quilt top, make sure that they get a tracking number for it. Have them either supply you with the tracking number or let you know when it will arrive, so you can keep an eye out for the package and let them know that it arrived safely. That way, if it takes longer than expected or doesn't show up, you can be in communication about it sooner rather than later.

When sending quilts through the mail, it's important to purchase insurance on the package. You can ask your client how much they want it insured for or estimate the value yourself. I've never had any problems shipping quilts through the mail (with any carrier), and I always tell myself that it's because I buy the insurance that I've never needed it! (Hope I didn't just jinx myself!)

For those quilts that can be picked up or delivered locally, try to choose only one or two days a week for this, to avoid constant disruption to your work schedule. If clients come to your house, let them know what day and time they can make their drop-offs and pickups. If you meet clients off-site, set up appointments with them and be on time. Try to do this on the same day that you might have packages to drop off to be mailed. Make one trip do it all. Time is money! Guard it carefully.

PERSONAL TOUCHES

It's the little personal touches that let you show your customers just how much you really do appreciate them.

"Never stop thinking about how to delight your customer." ~ **WARREN BUFFETT**

THERE ARE SEVERAL SIMPLE, INEXPENSIVE WAYS TO REWARD YOUR CUSTOMERS FOR CHOOSING YOU AS THEIR LONGARM QUILTER. HERE ARE A FEW:

* Give your customer's quilts back to them in a custom-printed tote bag.

* Offer free local pickup and delivery.

* Hand out coupons.

* Offer a Frequent Quilter program, such as a "baker's dozen" punch card ("Get 12 quilts quilted, get a discount on the 13th.") or another offer.

* Return the finished quilt with a free goodie with your contact information on it.

* Send a personalized thank-you note or gift. (I often send Victoria a bag of Coffee Nut M&M's!)

* Send your customers a numbered raffle ticket. Every so often, have a random drawing. Whoever holds the winning ticket gets a future discount or some other goodie!

* Offer gift certificates, so that anyone looking for a gift for their favorite quilter has options.

* One quilter in my area lets her customers choose a premade label for their quilt that they can personalize with their information and stitch to the back of their quilt. She also returns their quilts in a handmade pillowcase-type storage bag.

When you make your clients feel appreciated, they will be glad they chose you as their quilter. They'll keep returning and tell all their friends how happy they are with your work. That's the best advertising for your business you'll ever find.

CHAPTER 5

making the magic happen

YOU HAVE A ROAD MAP FOR HOW YOU'RE GOING TO OPERATE, YOU HAVE A FABULOUS LONGARM MACHINE, AND MOST IMPORTANTLY, you have customers who need your services. It's all good. But now what?

Now that you've gotten your business going, you have to actually get down to the day-to-day work of running your business. It ain't gonna run itself!

SETTING UP YOUR SPACE

Before you purchased your longarm machine, you learned how much space it would take up, and made sure that you had room for it in your studio—didn't you? Now that it's here and in place, it looks bigger than you thought it would, doesn't it?

And what about all the other stuff? You have to store thread, batting, customer quilts, and all your tools. And you need to be able to work conveniently and safely. Here are some things to think about.

Thread Storage

How will you store your thread? If you have more than one type of thread, you will probably want to keep like kinds together. Thread also needs to be kept out of direct sunlight to avoid fading and where dust won't collect on it. There are a lot of storage solutions, and what you choose will depend on the space you have and how much money you want to spend. For some great ideas, use the search term "longarm quilting thread storage" on Pinterest.

Batting Storage

Do you have a plan for storing all the batting you will need to keep on hand? My longarm studio has a nice closet that I use for all my batting storage. It holds several large rolls and packages of batting, and I even have a shelf to put scrap pieces on.

••• Some quilters keep their batting rolls on a bar underneath their longarm machine. Some have convenient wall racks to hold their rolls of batting. Search on Pinterest for "quilt batting storage ideas," and you will see a lot of great suggestions.

Tool Storage

YOU WILL WANT YOUR TOOLS TO BE EASILY ACCESSIBLE AND WITHIN REACH WHEN YOU ARE AT YOUR MACHINE. Consider mounting a couple small pegboards on the nearest walls with different types of hooks to hold rulers, scissors, and other items. Some shelving might be useful, as well—but if you mount shelving near your longarm, make sure it's not where you will bump your head on it while working!

A rolling cart (such as an IKEA Råskog utility cart) is super-handy for holding a lot of your most-often-used tools, and since it's on wheels, you can roll it around to wherever you need it.

Items you don't need to use as often can be stored in drawers or a cabinet. You'll need to store a lot of little things, such as extra needles, bobbins, and marking utensils, so consider baskets or drawer organizers to hold like items together and keep them from scattering.

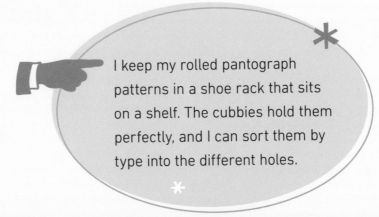

I keep my rolled pantograph patterns in a shoe rack that sits on a shelf. The cubbies hold them perfectly, and I can sort them by type into the different holes.

Customer Quilts

You will often have customer quilts in your possession awaiting their turn on your machine. The number of quilts you have will depend on your backlog, turnaround time, and insurance. (See Other People's Property, page 136, in Chapter 6.) You'll need a safe and convenient place to store these quilts.

MY BATTING CLOSET HAS A BAR IN IT, SO I BOUGHT STURDY HANGERS SO I COULD PUT MY CUSTOMER QUILTS ON HANGERS IN THE CLOSET. I clip the quilt's take-in form to its hanger.

Natalia Bonner, of Piece N Quilt, puts her customer quilts (and paperwork) in a custom tote bag, then hangs the tote on a hanger in a closet. When she returns the quilt to the customer, it goes back in the tote bag—a free gift!

OTHER LONGARMERS STORE CUSTOMER QUILTS IN BIG STORAGE TUBS. If you do this, be careful that the tubs don't allow light through the sides, so that the quilts are not exposed to sunlight. Also make sure to label everything carefully, so they don't get all mixed up in the tub. Imagine using one customer's backing or batting on another customer's quilt! Yikes!

Once quilts are finished, you need a safe place to keep them until you deliver them to the customers. Natalia's idea above would work for finished quilts as well. Most of my quilts get shipped in the mail, so I box them up right away, put them in a designated spot by the door, and ship them the same day or the next day. (For more information, see Shipping and Handling, page 99, in Chapter 4.)

If you have pets, be sure to store your customer quilts in a place the pets cannot access.

SCHEDULING

For me, the most difficult part of running a business of quilting for hire is the scheduling of customer jobs. Despite my good intentions, and my attempts at realistic estimates for the completion of any given job, something always comes up to derail me. Always.

••• The trick is to learn, over time, how to build things like this into your schedule and work around them. My Cowboy says, "The interruptions are never gonna go away. It's life. You have to learn how to roll with it." And he's so right. (Do *not* tell him I said that!)

WHEN ESTIMATING HOW LONG A PARTICULAR QUILT IS GOING TO TAKE, PAD IT BY AT LEAST 30%. When estimating how many quilts you can get done in a certain period of time, reduce it by about 40% of what you think you can do.

If you've been quilting for a while, you'll have some historical data you can review to see what you've been getting done and use that to plan your schedule going forward.

Your schedule will vary, depending on what type of quilting you do and how many hours you wish to work. Custom quilting usually takes a lot longer than doing a pantograph. A quick allover free-motion design can go really quickly, allowing you to do more quilts in less time.

I PERSONALLY AVERAGE ABOUT 100 QUILTS PER YEAR. That's about two quilts a week. I try to sprinkle some easier, quicker quilts in among all the highly custom jobs to give myself a break. Doing mostly custom work is very intense, so having a quilt that only needs a pantograph or a quick allover to squeeze in between custom quilts gives me a chance to rest and recover, so I can go on to the next custom quilt with a fresh outlook.

You may be able to do more than that, so you can adjust your schedule accordingly. You might want to do fewer than that, based on how you have your business set up.

Scheduling yourself too tightly is a recipe for anxiety and burnout, and it can compromise your commitment to superior customer service. I learned this the hard way. It took me a couple years to work myself out from under the overwhelming backlog and get my schedule back on track so I could meet deadlines for my customers. It's something I still struggle with.

Conversely, you need to make sure you're scheduling enough jobs to make the money that you need to make. If you financed your startup, you will have no choice but to do enough work to make enough money to cover your monthly loan payment. So you will have to schedule carefully to make sure you can do this. Your business plan (see Craft the Perfect Business Plan, page 43) can help you decide how many jobs you need.

YOU ALSO NEED TO BUILD SOME TIME INTO YOUR SCHEDULE TO PRACTICE. Work on a quilt of your own every once in a while, so you can try new things. If you hit a lull in your schedule and have a slow time coming up, that's a good time to practice. Plus, it will provide you with samples you can show off and use to attract more customers.

*

A lot of professional quilters, myself included, are often heard saying that they never get time to work on quilts of their own. You have to build it in to your schedule. My current policy is this: If my frame is empty on a weekend, then I can use it to load a quilt of my own. It makes me try harder to finish customer jobs by Friday afternoon, instead of procrastinating and telling myself that I have all weekend to get the customer quilt done. *

It's also not a bad idea if you just take a break from quilting during a slow period. It'll be good for you, prevent burnout, and leave you ready to come back refreshed.

There will inevitably be those customers who frantically call you up wanting a rush job. What do you do? Quilters are generally compassionate beings, so your first inclination is probably to juggle things around to accommodate them, but that may not be in your best interest. If they want something quick and simple, and you're in a good spot to help them out, then by all means, impart that good will, but charge a rush fee for it.

••• If it simply won't work into your schedule without throwing everything else in your schedule completely off track, then politely decline and tactfully explain your schedule to them, while encouraging them to give you more notice in the future, when you would be glad to help them out if you have enough advance notice. Refer them to another quilter in your vicinity, if at all possible.

ONE LAST IMPORTANT THING WHEN PLANNING YOUR SCHEDULE: TAKE INTO CAREFUL CONSIDERATION THOSE CLIENTS WHO HAVE IMPORTANT DEADLINES AND MAKE SURE THAT YOU CAN MEET THEM, ABOVE ALL ELSE. Designers often have nonnegotiable deadlines for submissions for books, magazines, trade shows, and exhibits. You do *not* want to be the cause of them missing an important deadline! And remember that shipping time needs to be included, and they will need time to bind the quilt and possibly have it photographed. Good communication is key in these instances. Do what you say you will, even if you have to work a lot of overtime to get it done.

NOTES

ORGANIZING YOUR TIME

If you're wearing all those hats you thought you would be when you worked your way through Chapter 1, then you're gonna be busy!

⟶ **You have to stay organized.**

⟶ **You have to protect your work schedule.**

⟶ **You have to stay focused.**

Sometimes you *think* you're doing all these things, when in reality, you're just spinning your wheels.

If you're just starting out, it will take some time to work out the kinks and get things all set up and running smoothly, but as you work, you will figure out what needs to be fixed, adjusted, done away with, or changed. It will get easier with time.

Time Log: A Week in the Life ...

A good place to start is to realistically figure out how you're spending your time in any given week. It may not be the way you think. How will you do this? Fill out a time log!

There is a downloadable Time Log form available (see Downloads, page 10)—so you can print it out as many times as you need to.

THE TIME LOG WE'LL BE USING IS SET UP FOR AN 8 TO 5 WORKDAY (AND I PUT A LUNCH HOUR IN THERE FOR YOU, BECAUSE IT'S IMPORTANT). Your schedule may not be 8 to 5, or you may be only part time. That's okay. Be sure to indicate on your Time Log the hours you have scheduled for your work. This is *your* Time Log. It won't look like mine or anyone else's!

TIME LOG

TIME	MONDAY	TUESDAY	WEDNESDAY	THURSDAY	FRIDAY
8:00					
8:30					
9:00					
9:30					
10:00					
10:30					
11:00					
11:30					
12:00	Lunch hour: What happens on lunch hour stays on lunch hour! This time is your own. Take it—you need a break!				
12:30					
1:00					
1:30					
2:00					
2:30					
3:00					
3:30					
4:00					
4:30					

HERE'S WHAT TO DO WITH IT:

We'll start on a Monday. As you go through your day, start plugging in the things you are *actually* doing. Write down everything you do in the time slot you did it in.

Try to fill it in as you go through your day; for instance, every hour or so. This way you don't get to the end of the day and have to try and remember everything you did that day or you *will* forget some things that need to be written down. Put everything you do for your workday on this sheet. Keep this log for an entire Monday through Friday workweek. You can see my sample Time Log to see how that really goes for me (and start to wonder how I actually get anything done)!

SAMPLE TIME LOG

TIME	MONDAY	TUESDAY	WEDNESDAY	THURSDAY	FRIDAY
8:00	Do laundry, drink coffee, answer emails, fill orders	Computer time	Wash dishes, drink coffee, answer emails, do paperwork, fill orders, talk to my dad on the phone	Computer time, writing blog post, writing pattern instructions	Computer time
8:30	Desk time: weekly review/ plan my week				
9:00		Coffee break, check goats, do laundry, console a cat	Etsy shop maintenance, website updates		Binding a quilt
9:30	Load a customer quilt on the longarm	Run the longarm			
10:00			Run the longarm	Machine piecing	
10:30	Coffee break, check goats, check on My Cowboy, referee a cat fight, chat with the mail lady, plan supper, search for embroidery stabilizer, attempt to organize some of my fabric scraps				Coffee break, check goats, talk to my dad, have a snack, chat with the mail lady, move some piles around in the name of "cleaning," fuss with the printer, attempt to clean off my desk
11:00					
11:30					
12:00	Lunch hour: What happens on lunch hour stays on lunch hour! This time is your own. Take it—you need a break!				
12:30					
1:00	Run the longarm	Run the longarm	Let lunch hour run over	Run the longarm	Run the longarm
1:30			Run the longarm		
2:00					
2:30		Check goats, eat popcorn, watch an episode of *Hoarders*			

Time				
3:00	Short break	Power nap		Short break, try and find an excuse to knock off early, but let common sense prevail
3:30	Run the longarm	Run the longarm	Load a customer quilt on the longarm	Run the longarm
4:00				
4:30		Standing and staring		

Now, it's time to analyze this important and revealing document!

HERE ARE SOME QUESTIONS TO ASK YOURSELF:

How many hours did I spend actually doing real work related to my business? _____

How many hours were spent doing things not work related? _____

Could any of those things have been done at another time? In other words, were they nonurgent tasks? _____

When I am doing real work-related activities, am I spending my time on the right things? _____

Are most of the things I'm doing earning my business money or otherwise benefiting my business? _____

If something took longer than I thought it would, why did it? Did I have too many interruptions? Was I not fully prepared? Unable to focus? Or did I simply underestimate the time it would take?

_____

_____

Are there any really important things I needed to do that I didn't have time for?

_____

_____

What things can I eliminate?

_____

_____

Are there things I'm doing that I can delegate or hire out? What are they?

_____

Will hiring these things out help me make more money or simply cost me more money? _____

Am I wasting time? _____

Where can I improve? _____

Now that you know where you're spending time, you can come up with ways to do better the next week. Or you may already be a Time-Management Rock Star and don't need to change a thing!

IF YOU'RE LIKE ME, IT MIGHT BEHOOVE YOU TO FILL OUT ANOTHER TIME LOG FOR THE NEXT WEEK, ANALYZE IT AGAIN IN THE SAME FASHION, AND SEE IF YOU ARE IMPROVING AT FOCUSING ON WHAT YOU REALLY NEED TO GET DONE, AND LEAVING OUT THE UNIMPORTANT THINGS. Keep your work time for work, and do your personal and family stuff outside your regular work schedule. Much easier said than done!

••• I actually do quite a bit of work outside of normal work hours, on weekends and in the evenings, which evens out with the way I let personal stuff spill over into my working hours. I find it super-difficult to avoid this when working from home! I also make the most of my early-morning time and my lunch hours to do a lot of little things. And I like to break the longarming sessions into chunks, because standing at the machine for hours on end is physically hard. Those breaks are important.

You may feel you need to redo a Time Log every so often, just to keep yourself on track and to make sure unimportant fluff isn't creeping back into your schedule. You may find things that need to be added, taken out, or rearranged. Keep tweaking it as you go. It will change over time, and that's normal. Use it to get yourself back on track and to help you stay focused and get the important work of your business done.

AND—MAKE THE MOST OF YOUR NONWORK TIME! ENJOY IT TO THE FULLEST.

DOING THE WORK

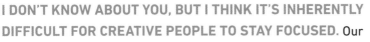

"There's no substitute for hard work."

~ THOMAS A. EDISON

I DON'T KNOW ABOUT YOU, BUT I THINK IT'S INHERENTLY DIFFICULT FOR CREATIVE PEOPLE TO STAY FOCUSED. Our minds are always working on new ideas and jumping ahead to the next shiny, new thing. And here's the big one for me: Once I know how something is going to turn out, I get bored with it and want to move on. Next!

So when I'm quilting a quilt that has what seems like 140 blocks all requiring the same design quilted on them (when, really, it's only 20 blocks), or when I've spent an entire hour quilting a little 4-inch area of a large quilt, it's really difficult for me to not get bored and walk away. Repetition is an attention-span killer! I can come up with a million excuses for other things to do instead: I need to scoop the litter box, check my email, throw in a load of laundry, wash the dishes, check on the goats,... the possibilities are endless!

Then, too, there is the day-to-day grind. Wake up, make the coffee, run the longarm,... day after day after day. I like to have more than that to look forward to—how about you?

••• Burnout is real, and if you don't take that into consideration, your mojo will leave the building and you'll have a hard time convincing it to come back. And you have customers who are expecting you to be working—some of them have deadlines!

How to Stay Motivated

"Learn to master the mundane." ~ **DARREN HARDY**

You know you need to do the work—so how do you stay on track and keep from getting distracted?

CREATE GAMES

A favorite way to keep myself on track is making things into a game. If I have several things on my to-do list, and find myself procrastinating, I use Random Number Generator (random.org) to choose one for me. I can't argue with the number—I have to do that task before I can move on! (My friends make fun of me, but it really does work.)

I get distracted so easily, it's ridiculous. My longarm used to be in our living room. One day I heard My Cowboy starting a movie. We both knew I needed to be working, but I still asked, "What movie are we watching?", thinking I'd sort of listen to it as I worked. He quipped back, "I think it's called *Silence of the Longarm*."

Another time, I heard music, and asked, "Are we watchin' a movie?"

"Nope."

"Oh," I said. "I thought you were startin' a movie."

He shot back, "And I thought you were startin' to work. I guess we're both surprised!"

Now I work upstairs, and he can't tell when I'm getting distracted!

USE A TIMER

I set a timer for a certain amount of time and tell myself I have to stay on task *only* until it rings, and then I can take a break or spend a few minutes on something else. My daddy always says, "Getting started is the hardest part!" Often, by the time the timer goes off, I've hit my groove and can just keep on working.

REWARD YOURSELF

✳ Finish a job and have some chocolate.

✳ Check a big task off your to-do list and go pet a goat!

✳ Meet a big deadline and schedule a massage—or simply take a few hours off.

✳ Get everything on your list done for the week, so you can sew on projects of your own with the time you have left...

✳ ...or get a head start on the next week to alleviate some of that upcoming workload.

GIVE YOURSELF A DEADLINE

Set your own self-imposed deadlines. Even if it's not true, tell yourself that Job X must be done by a certain date. Use backward planning to figure out how much you need to do each day to meet that goal, and then make sure you get that much done each day. Reward yourself for meeting the goal. Give yourself an even bigger reward if you get done early!

USE THE POMODORO TECHNIQUE

DEVELOPED BY FRANCESCO CIRILLO, THE POMODORO TECHNIQUE CONSISTS OF SIX MAIN STEPS:

1. Choose a task.

2. Set a timer for 25 minutes.

3. Work on the task for 25 uninterrupted minutes.

4. Give yourself a check mark for making it through the session.

5. Take a short break.

6. Do it again. After every four sessions, give yourself a longer break.

USE FOCUS BLOCKS

A focus block is a dedicated period of time that you set aside to work on a task without any interruptions or distractions. Ideally, you will want to schedule your focus blocks when you're at your best, not when you're lagging or tired. You might use your Time Log to see when you can best schedule yourself some focus blocks.

OTHER IDEAS

I ASKED FELLOW LONGARM QUILTERS HOW THEY STAY MOTIVATED AND INSPIRED. HERE ARE A FEW OF THEIR ANSWERS:

Look at quilts on Instagram.

Go to guild meetings.

Watch YouTube instructional videos.

Do something different, such as knitting, crochet, or (gasp) housecleaning!

Work on a different quilting project, so you have more variety in your quilting activity.

Take a break.

Take a day off.

Fake it till you make it. Power through, and just keep going, even when you don't want to.

Clean up and organize your studio.

Look at quilting books or magazines.

Take a week off.

Get together with quilting friends for a retreat or sew day.

Put on your favorite music and get to work!

Visit a quilt shop.

What are some other ways you can keep yourself motivated?

_____

_____

_____

_____

If you're struggling because you're overwhelmed, take a closer look at how you're scheduling yourself and make some adjustments. Your Time Log might come in handy here. Revise your quilting schedule, build in a bit of down time, communicate any changes with your clients who might be affected, take a deep breath, and start over.

Ice cream always helps, too!

And this brings me to our next topic. ...

Self-Care

You *must* take care of yourself. If you are the only person running your business, then you are fully aware that if you aren't working, your business is probably not making any money. No one pays you for sick days, personal time off, or vacations.

If you've been overworking yourself, build some self-care activities into your routine. *Bonus:* Some of these might also help with motivation!

HERE ARE A FEW IDEAS:

→ Get enough exercise.

→ Stay hydrated.

→ Get plenty of rest.

→ Take real lunch breaks.

→ Schedule a day out with friends or a shopping day.

→ Take a coffee break. Even better if it's with a friend.

→ Enjoy a bubble bath or a nice, long, hot shower.

→ Do something creative that is different from what you usually do.

→ Spend time outdoors. Pet a goat!

→ Get a massage.

→ Try breathing exercises or meditation.

→ Watch something funny on TV.

→ Read.

→ Treat yourself. (May I suggest ice cream?)

CHAPTER 6

money, money, money

MONEY: IT COMES IN, IT GOES OUT. And you need to keep good track of it, so you know if your business is doing well or not. We all hope for smooth sailing and a steady income, but as a professional quilter for hire, your cash flow will depend on your schedule, and you have to be aware that there will be slow times and unexpected expenses along the way. You also need to plan ahead so you will be able to pay your taxes on time. And don't forget insurance. In this chapter, we're going to talk about all that!

SETTING PRICES

Pricing is a topic of concern for many professional quilters. It is discussed hard and often. And you'll probably never be done worrying over it.

How do I charge?

_____

_____

_____

_____

What do I charge?

_____

_____

_____

_____

Am I charging enough?

_____

_____

_____

_____

When should I raise my prices?

_____

_____

_____

_____

Should I offer discounts?

_____

_____

_____

_____

What is my minimum fee?

_____

_____

_____

_____

How much am I actually making per hour?

_____

_____

_____

_____

"Earning a living wage takes a ton of confidence that most people don't have. What would you like to make at a 'normal' job? Wouldn't it be nice to make that as a quilter?" ~ **KAREN MCTAVISH, OF MCTAVISH QUILTING STUDIO**

Most quilters charge for their quilting services by the square inch. The price per square inch varies according to the complexity of the quilting service desired. A simple allover meander would be the lowest price, and heirloom custom quilting would be the highest, with other levels falling somewhere in between. Common prices can range from 1 cent per square inch for an easy allover, to 1.5 to 2.5 cents per square inch for a pantograph. Custom quilting can start at 3 cents per inch, and go up to as high as 10 cents per square inch (or even more) for the most intricate custom designs by the best professionals. How much you charge will depend on your level of experience and how long you've been at it.

As you work, pay attention to how many hours it takes you to finish a quilt in all the different ways you do quilting. Take into consideration how long it takes you to prep and load the quilt before you can even begin. Time yourself as you perform the other services you offer, so that you don't shortchange yourself by doing someone's binding by hand for $3 and a pat on the back. This will help you price all your services.

YOU WILL SOON LEARN HOW LONG EACH TYPE OF JOB TAKES YOU TO COMPLETE, AND YOU WILL HAVE SOME DATA TO USE FOR FIGURING UP AND DECIDING IF YOU ARE CHARGING ENOUGH, OR IF YOU NEED TO RAISE YOUR PRICES. Divide the amount of money you charged the customer by the number of hours you spent to complete the job. That is your hourly wage.

HERE ARE A COUPLE EXAMPLES....

CUSTOMER A:

She hired you to quilt an 84″ × 100″ quilt with an easy custom design. She supplied her own batting and backing.

Setup and prep took 1 hour.

You spent 10 hours on the custom quilting, which was mostly freehand quilting with a little bit of stitch-in-the-ditch work using a straight-edge ruler, for a total of 11 hours.

You charged 3.5 cents per square inch, for a total of $294.

Divide the total dollar amount ($294) by the total number of hours you spent (11 hours), and you made $26.73 per hour for this job. Not so bad!

CUSTOMER B:

He hired you to quilt a 60″ × 80″ T-shirt quilt with an allover meander. He supplied his own backing and purchased the batting from you.

Setup and prep took 45 minutes (0.75 hour).

You spent 2 hours on the quilting.

You charged 1.5 cents per square inch—your lowest price for the easiest type of quilting—for a total of $72.

Divide the total dollar amount ($72) by the total number of hours you spent (2.75 hours), and you made $26.18 per hour, plus a bit of profit from the sale of the batting. Still not horrible! That's a fairly tolerable skilled-labor wage.

Every job will be different, and you need to pay attention to what types of work you're doing at what price to make sure you're making a living wage. You don't want to work for less than you would pay someone else doing the same job—look out for yourself. If you don't like what you're making per hour, then you need to adjust your pricing to bring it up to what you need to be making. And don't forget: You need to be able to pay your bills!

Some quilters charge by the square foot instead of the square inch, but I feel that the math is much easier if you price by the square inch.

Some quilters simply charge by the hour to ensure that they're earning the hourly wage they want to make. If you've been quilting for a while, then you may have a good idea of how long a certain type of quilting will take you on a quilt of a certain size, so that you know how to estimate that cost for a client. You also need to be able to carefully track your time with this method. This method doesn't work for me because I get distracted way too easily!

YOU ALSO NEED TO SET A MINIMUM CHARGE FOR EACH TYPE OF QUILTING YOU DO, SO THAT A SMALL QUILT DOESN'T EAT UP TOO MUCH TIME FOR VERY LITTLE COMPENSATION. It takes time to load a quilt, get everything set up, and choose thread before you ever even start the quilting. A minimum charge will ensure that you're getting paid for that nonquilting time you spend, even when the quilting part doesn't take very long.

If there are other quilters in your area, don't price yourself beneath them just to undercut their prices. But by the same token, if you're just starting out, don't price yourself the same as the most highly experienced quilter in your area that is doing custom heirloom work and has been at it for twenty years.

AS YOU GAIN EXPERIENCE, AND GET BETTER AND BETTER AT WHAT YOU DO, IT'S WISE TO RAISE YOUR PRICES. When is it time? Well, if you're quilting full time, you're gaining a lot of experience over the course of a year. Chances are, you're getting faster at finishing quilts, so if you charge by the hour, you might actually be making less money per quilt—so that would be a good reason to raise your prices every so often.

I usually evaluate my pricing at the beginning of every year. Sometimes, raising prices means simply rearranging my categories so that certain types of quilting fall into the next highest bracket. Other times, it's an actual total pricing makeover. Some years, I don't make any changes at all.

Karen McTavish, of McTavish Quilting Studio, says that you need not fear that you will lose customers by raising your prices. You most likely will not lose any, and even if you do, you'll be making more money per quilt, even if you're doing fewer quilts, so it will even out.

JUST REMEMBER: THERE IS NO PERFECT FORMULA, AND YOU CAN MAKE ADJUSTMENTS AS YOU GO.

ACCOUNTING CONCERNS

Since you *are* a legitimate business and not a hobby anymore, careful records of income and expenses need to be kept for tax purposes. These records will be helpful when updating your business plan (see tip, page 44), and they will alert you to whether you're doing as well as you'd like to be doing, in case you need to make adjustments.

EVEN IF YOU HIRE AN ACCOUNTANT TO DO YOUR BOOKKEEPING, YOU STILL HAVE TO DO CAREFUL RECORDKEEPING, BECAUSE ONCE YOU HAND IT ALL OFF, YOUR ACCOUNTANT NEEDS TO BE ABLE TO MAKE SENSE OF IT. And did you know that they want details? I often joke that I do more paperwork since I hired an accountant than I did before!

If you're doing it all yourself, then you are the one who will need to make sense of it all, especially at tax time.

My friend Becky Collis, of Collis Country Quilting, does her own bookkeeping. She keeps a record of all her income in the same log book that she uses for scheduling her customer quilts.

Karyn Dornemann, of KarynQuilts, also does her own bookkeeping by using QuickBooks Desktop software.

However you decide to handle all the bookkeeping that comes along with your business, I have found that if you group your expenses into a set number of categories, then they're a lot easier to sort out when the time rolls around to deal with them. If you have hired an accountant, ask for advice on how you should categorize things. The more organized you are when you hand them your paperwork, the less it will cost you for their bookkeeping services!

HERE ARE THE CATEGORIES MY ACCOUNTANT HAS SET UP FOR ME....

Advertising and promotion	Postage and shipping
Donations	Printing
Dues and subscriptions	Professional fees
Entry fees	Repairs and maintenance
Interest and penalties	Supplies
Labor	Taxes
Meals and entertainment	Training
Merchant license	Travel
Office supplies	Website expenses

There are various ways you can keep track of everything. For some software programs that you might find helpful, check Resources (page 205). If you're using a paper system, purchase a ledger book to record everything in, and set a time to do it regularly.

WHATEVER YOU DO, DO *NOT* PUT IT OFF. When you come to the end of the year without having paid any attention to your paperwork, it will be nearly impossible to remember what you did back in January or February if you can't make sense of your notes or didn't provide enough detail.

Do your paperwork at least once a month, while things are still fairly fresh in your mind. Build a desk day into your schedule each month, or set aside an hour or two every week, so you won't feel that you don't have time for it. When tax time comes around, you will be so glad you did!

TAXES

The types of taxes you will need to pay may depend on the type of business entity you have chosen for yourself, so be sure to check with an accountant or a tax professional to make sure you're not forgetting something important. Incurring a penalty for failing to file the proper returns will cause you grief you don't need to deal with.

Sales Tax

YOU WILL NEED TO FILE A SALES TAX RETURN, SO THAT YOU CAN REMIT TO THE STATE THE SALES TAX YOU HAVE COLLECTED FROM THE SALE OF ITEMS TO YOUR CUSTOMERS, SUCH AS BATTING, THREAD, BACKING, OR ANY OTHER PRODUCTS. Depending on how much you make, this could be quarterly, but for small businesses like this, it is usually only yearly.

Property Tax

Some states charge property taxes on business equipment. Check with your local county assessor's office to see if any of your equipment is subject to property taxes. You will have to file an assessment form annually (usually at the beginning of the year), and then pay the appropriate taxes annually (usually at the end of that same year).

Income Tax

PLAN TO PAY PERSONAL INCOME TAXES ON YOUR EARNINGS, WHICH INCLUDES FEDERAL, STATE, AND SELF-EMPLOYMENT TAX (AND SOME-TIMES LOCAL INCOME TAX). Self-employment tax gets calculated on the tax return, and it includes your obligation to Social Security. As a self-employed person, you will want to work closely with your accountant so they can figure out your quarterly estimated tax payments, which is how you should pay income tax. Making quarterly payments is easier and less of a burden than having to come up with a huge lump sum payment every April, and you can avoid a penalty by paying quarterly.

Inventory

If you keep items in your inventory that you sell to your clients, you will need to have a full accounting of the items in your possession at the end of every year. The value of your inventory for tax purposes is based on your cost for the items, not what you charge for retail.

FINANCIAL CONCERNS

Collecting Money

MOST QUILTERS REQUIRE THAT THE JOBS THEY DO ARE PAID FOR BEFORE THE QUILT IS RETURNED TO THE CUSTOMER. In the case of quilts getting shipped in the mail, you need to decide if you will require the payment to be in your hands before you ship the quilt, or if you're willing to go ahead and ship the quilt and trust that the client will pay in a timely manner.

If the customer is happy with your work, they should also be happy to pay you. After all, they will want to remain in good standing so they can hire you again. However, if you do end up with a client who is slow to pay, you may need to send a tactful reminder that their invoice is overdue.

If you're doing a high-dollar custom job, you may wish to require a deposit up front. Then you can collect the remaining balance when the quilt is finished.

Spending Money

If possible, it's a good idea to have a little money set aside for times when cash flow becomes an issue. In the event of an expensive equipment breakdown, you have to factor in both the expense of the repair and the time that you won't be able to work while your machine is out of commission.

You also need to take into account that you need to periodically order supplies, overhead expenses may vary with the seasons, and you might have underestimated how long some jobs will take, and therefore, you may not have as much money coming in as there is going out.

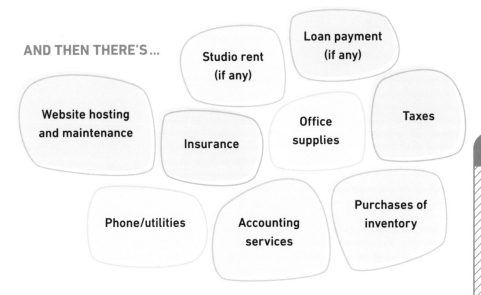

AND THEN THERE'S...

Studio rent (if any)

Loan payment (if any)

Website hosting and maintenance

Insurance

Office supplies

Taxes

Phone/utilities

Accounting services

Purchases of inventory

You need to keep careful records of your expenses. Get receipts for everything business related—and make sure to hang onto them!

> *"I keep a punch bowl full of receipts."*
> ~ **BECKY COLLIS, OF COLLIS COUNTRY QUILTING**

For receipts that don't have a lot of information on them, I write directly on the receipt what it was for, so I can be sure it gets into the proper expense category. My accountant also really likes it if I indicate the method I used for payment: cash, debit card, PayPal, and so on.

IF YOU USE YOUR BUSINESS CREDIT CARD, BE SURE TO KEEP IT PAID PROMPTLY, SO THAT YOU ARE BUILDING A GOOD CREDIT RECORD FOR YOUR BUSINESS. And if you have loan payments, don't be late with them! It's easy to let your credit record fall, but very difficult to bring it back up.

INSURANCE

Your business needs insurance.

It will greatly help your peace of mind and alleviate a lot of worry.

What kind of insurance? That will depend on a few things.

Check with your insurance agent. Every insurance company varies, so you may want to comparison shop among the insurance companies in your area to see what your options are. Plus, it's always good to get more than one quote so that you can compare them and get the coverage you desire for the best possible price.

You should also do a periodic review of your policy to make sure that things are still in order and that your coverage is still current. If you pay your premiums annually, each year just before it becomes due would be a good time to review it. Don't let it slide and end up caught between a rock and a hard place, should something happen!

What Do I Need To Insure?

There are four main parts of your business that you need to protect: building, business property, other people's property, and yourself.

BUILDING

If your business is in your house, your regular homeowner's policy will cover the building.

IF YOUR BUSINESS IS IN YOUR HOUSE, BUT YOU RENT YOUR HOME, THEN YOU MAY HAVE RENTER'S INSURANCE; HOWEVER, THIS WILL USUALLY ONLY COVER PERSONAL BELONGINGS. To insure your business in your rented home, it may require a separate Business in the Home policy or rider, so be sure to check with your agent.

If your business is in a separate building from your house, but on the same property, you will need to make sure the building is insured, either with your primary homeowner's policy or with a separate policy for your business.

If your business is in an off-site studio owned by you, you will need to insure the building. If you rent or lease the space from someone else, then the responsibility of insuring the building itself is not on you, but you should definitely double-check to make sure the landlord does indeed have the building insured.

BUSINESS PROPERTY

Your business has a lot of important items that need to be covered. First and foremost, your longarm machine(s), which can cost anywhere from $5,000 to $50,000. If something happened to that machine, you'd pretty much be out of business, right?

You most likely have a regular sewing machine as well (or more than one), which can cost anywhere from $200 to $20,000 (or more). You may have a specialty machine, such as an embroidery machine or a serger, too. Important property to cover.

And what about all your tools and supplies? Be sure to keep track of batting, thread, fabric, tools and equipment used with your machines, tools and equipment used in your daily work, your books and patterns, and even your computer and printer.

Some insurance companies may require you to create and maintain a basic inventory of all your business property to help them calculate the value of a loss, should one occur.

OTHER PEOPLE'S PROPERTY

Here's a biggie! What about all the customer quilts you have in your possession that are waiting in line to be worked on by you? You need to make sure they are covered. Some policies will cover them simply because they are considered to be in your "care and custody," but you need to make sure. In other instances, there may be a limit to the total value of customer quilts that will be covered. You need to know what that is and try never to keep more than that in your possession. And you will most likely need to have an inventory of what these are in order to make a claim.

YOURSELF

• • • Liability insurance is really important. Your primary homeowner's policy most likely has liability insurance included, since it's such an important type of coverage. But if clients are coming to your house to pick up or drop off quilts, take lessons, or any other business activity, you need to make sure that you have liability insurance to cover any risks inherent with that. You don't want a customer tripping on your doorstep, breaking an ankle, and then suing you for all the medical bills!

If you are renting your home, it is in your best interest to purchase your own liability insurance along with your renter's and business policies. If a client falls down your stairs and breaks a leg, the liability is yours, *unless* you can prove that the landlord was negligent for some reason. For example, if you asked the landlord to install a handrail or repair the steps, and the landlord did not do it, then the responsibility is on the landlord; but if such is not the case, and you merely have a clumsy client, then the responsibility is yours. It's best to protect yourself.

THIS TYPE OF COVERAGE WILL ALSO VARY DEPENDING ON THE TYPE OF BUSINESS ENTITY YOU HAVE CHOSEN. If you are a Sole Proprietorship, you may need more coverage than if you are set up as an LLC, since your personal assets could be at risk. Check with your agent to make sure you have enough coverage in this area.

How Do I Need To Insure It?

RIDER OR ENDORSEMENT

Some companies allow you to simply add a rider to your current home-owner's policy that will cover your business. A rider (also sometimes called an endorsement) is a provision that adds benefits to or amends the terms of your basic insurance policy to cover additional things not included in your primary policy. If your policy allows a rider for business property coverage, make sure that it includes all the parts of your business that you want to insure.

••• If you rent your home, make sure that your business is covered in its own policy or rider, in addition to your Renter's Insurance that covers your personal belongings.

COMMERCIAL BUSINESS POLICY

THIS MAY BE CALLED ANY NUMBER OF SIMILAR THINGS, AND EACH COMPANY WILL HAVE DIFFERENT RULES AND COVERAGES, BUT THIS IS BASICALLY A SEPARATE INSURANCE POLICY THAT IS STRICTLY TO COVER YOUR BUSINESS. You can insure all the things stated above, or pick and choose what you may need. For instance, if your business is in your house, and your house is already covered through homeowner's insurance, you won't need to insure a building, but you will still need to cover your business property. If you rent your home, then you will need to insure your business property in addition to your personal belongings, most likely in separate policies.

Most policies have a set list of "named perils" that they will cover. Familiarize yourself with what these are, and make sure your policy covers, at the very least, the ones you might be in danger of. Depending on where you live, you could be in danger of a tornado, hurricane, landslide, earthquake, or raging wildfire. Theft and vandalism are usually covered. Note that while water damage may be covered, actual flooding from groundwater will most likely not be one of the named perils, so it will require extra coverage. (Thank goodness we live on top of a hill!)

Just be sure to check all this carefully.

IF YOUR LIABILITY INSURANCE PROVIDES GOOD ENOUGH COVERAGE AND INCLUDES COVERAGE FOR VISITS BY CUSTOMERS, THEN YOU WON'T HAVE TO INCLUDE THAT IN YOUR SEPARATE BUSINESS POLICY. This is sometimes called an Exclusion for Business Exposure, which is added on to your primary homeowner's policy (double-check to make sure!). If you rent your home, you will need to purchase your own liability insurance, or make sure it is included in your Business in the Home policy.

Don't be afraid to ask questions and shop around with different providers. Be sure you're getting the coverage you need, but not unnecessarily paying twice for something that is already covered.

Some agents I spoke with said that to insure your business in your home, you don't have to even have your home insured first, but they do recommend it. Some said you do have to have your home insured first, which is definitely the case if all you're doing is adding a rider. Some said you do need homeowner's insurance, but that your business policy does not necessarily have to be with the same insurance company. See how confusing this can get? Have a heart-to-heart with an agent you trust, and then shop around for the coverage that is best for you.

"Different people have different tolerances for risk." ~ **KEITH MORRISSEY, STATE FARM AGENT IN MACON, MISSOURI**

ONLY *YOU* CAN DECIDE HOW COMFORTABLE YOU ARE WITH THE LEVEL OF COVERAGE YOU ARE CARRYING.

YOU'RE PAYING FOR PEACE OF MIND!

CHAPTER 7
marketing

IN CHAPTER 3, I TALKED ABOUT BUILDING YOUR BRAND (page 74). Now that you have that done, it's time to put it to work! You need to put yourself out there and promote your business—even if it's scary or you're shy.

I also talked about establishing your online presence (page 77), so be sure you've done your work there—since having an online presence is of particular importance to a business of any kind these days.

> *"Ya need to toot yer own horn, 'cause no one else is gonna do it for ya."*
> ~ MY COWBOY

INCREASING YOUR AUDIENCE

You need to get your work in front of those who matter. You need to get your business name out into the world, so that people will recognize it and want to hire you.

What makes you special?_____

_____

_____

_____

What can you do that no one else does? _____

_____

_____

_____

Is there a special service you provide that you want to be known for?

_____

_____

_____

Are there any current trends you can take advantage of? _____

_____

_____

_____

Go back and review Define Your Vision (page 27), in Chapter 2, for your business, and make sure that the marketing you want to do aligns with how you want to show up in the quilting world. This may evolve as you gain more experience, and that's okay.

••• Talk about and promote the types of quilting you want to do and what you want to be known for. If you don't like doing pantographs, don't promote that. If custom is your thing, then that's the thing you want to talk about and promote. You will attract the things you are promoting because that's what people will see and hear about you, and they will want those services.

HERE ARE A FEW WAYS TO PROMOTE YOURSELF:

✷ Keep your website current and your blog active. (More on this at the end of this chapter.)

✷ Join online groups where you can show your work. Some groups allow you to promote yourself and your business, and some don't, so follow the rules and always be nice. Even if you can't use the group for promotion, you can study the work of others to improve yourself, and you can learn a lot from fellow group members. It's also nice if you can offer to help with someone else's dilemma once in a while. Some groups have a directory where you can get your business's name listed, so when someone in your area is looking for a quilter, your name will pop up as a possible quilter for hire.

✷ Check to see if there are any online directories where you can get your business listed, so when someone is doing an online search for a machine quilter in their area, your business will be on the list. If it gets you one customer, and that customer spreads the word, and so on, you will be glad you took the time to add yourself to the directory. These listings are usually free.

Do you have any designer customers? If something you quilt for one of your clients gets featured in a magazine or book, that's good exposure.

Speaking of exposure, however, do *not* accept work that you are doing solely in exchange for publicity. You deserve to be paid appropriately for the work you do. If you can determine that the exposure you will get in exchange for the work you do is worth it, then by all means go ahead, but consider carefully, so that you are not coming out on the losing end of the deal.

> "*A friend of mine once said, within earshot of My Cowboy, 'Exposure doesn't pay the bills.' To which My Cowboy immediately responded, 'Wait. I know plenty of people who would pay you to expose yourself!'* " ~ AUTHOR

BE PICKY ABOUT YOUR "EXPOSURE"!

MAKING CONNECTIONS

AS YOU GAIN MORE EXPERIENCE, AND WORD OF MOUTH GARNERS YOU MORE AND MORE CUSTOMERS, DON'T BE AFRAID TO REACH OUT TO THOSE WHO MIGHT HELP YOU GROW EVEN FURTHER.

Is there someone in your guild who's very prolific and needs another quilter to help them turn out quilts faster? If you have a fast turn-around on pantograph patterns, let them know you're available, what the turnaround time is, and that you can help them out.

Quilters who do computerized pantographs with a fast turnaround are able to stay consistently busy, which really helps the cash flow situation!

Is there someone in your guild or quilting circle who makes the type of quilt you'd love to get your hands on and apply your magic to? Approach them, and let them know you're available if they ever need a machine quilter. Hand them a business card and brochure at your guild meeting. If you show your own work at guild meetings, then fellow members who like your work will probably approach you first. Be ready.

POST YOUR WORK REGULARLY ON ALL YOUR SOCIAL MEDIA CHANNELS. It's like building up an online portfolio that potential customers can look at any time. Your dream client might just find you that way!

Is there a particular big-name designer that you'd like to quilt for? Follow them on social media. Don't be stalkerish, but do leave relevant comments now and then. If, after engaging with them for a while on social media, you still want to work with them, pop them a courteous email letting them know that your services are available. They may agree that you're a good match and may consider you as their quilter for hire in the near future. Be sure to provide them with links to places where they can look at your work. They need to see for themselves what you can do, especially if their work is high-profile or entered into competitions or exhibits regularly.

••• Don't be disappointed or discouraged if you get rejected or ignored at first. It takes time to build up a good reputation. Keep trying.

Good quilters who can meet the tight deadlines that designers usually have are in high demand. Position yourself as someone who can do the work and meet the deadlines, and word will spread.

ATTEND QUILT SHOWS AND PASS OUT BUSINESS CARDS. Go to the semiannual trade show for the quilting industry (Quilt Market) and network like crazy for a few days. You may come away with more work than you can shake a stick at!

Where I live, in Missouri, there is an organization called the Heartland Quilt Network. This organization is for quilt guilds, quilt shops, and quilting professionals and covers Missouri, Kansas, Nebraska, Iowa, Oklahoma, and Arkansas. It's a great way to network and promote yourself, if you're in one of these states. If you are not in one of these states, check to see if there is a similar organization in your area.

ADVERTISING

When I first got my machine, the lady that had previously been quilting my quilts for me told me, "Don't ever advertise, or you'll get more business than you can handle." She was actually quite right. Ask any professional longarm quilter worth their salt how far out their backlog is. It's usually several months, with a waiting list.

BUT WHEN YOU'RE FIRST STARTING OUT, YOU *DO* NEED TO LET PEOPLE KNOW THAT YOU'RE OPEN FOR BUSINESS. HERE ARE SOME EASY AND INEXPENSIVE WAYS TO DO THAT.

* **Pass out your business cards at quilt shows or other quilting events.**

* **Rent booth space at a local show.**

* **If you're in a quilt guild, make an announcement at your meeting. Pass out cards and brochures to your fellow guild members.**

* **If you're not in a guild, see if you can find one to join.**

* **Ask if you can leave some business cards in all your local quilt shops (or post a flyer).**

* **Post on all your social media accounts that you're taking in new customers.**

* **Ask your current customers to refer you to all their quilting friends.**

* **See if your local chamber of commerce can help you out, especially if you're a member.**

MEDIA

••• Don't discount traditional forms of media as a way to spread the word about your business. If you are ever invited to be on a podcast, be featured in a newspaper article, appear in a video or on a TV program, or have your work published in a magazine, consider doing it. Some of these will be paid appearances, some will not. You will have to carefully weigh the time you will spend doing it against the reward or compensation you will receive from doing it. Paid or not, sometimes it's just fun, and you'd be doing what you were doing anyway—so why not?

A friend of mine (and her quilt) made the front page of *The Paducah Sun* during AQS Quilt Week in Paducah, Kentucky, one year. I've appeared on local TV simply by being in attendance at a quilt show. We would both have been where we were, doing what we were doing, anyway, so why not take the publicity?

My dream client, Victoria Findlay Wolfe, was featured in the PBS award-winning series *Craft in America* in the episode on quilts. My work featured heavily in her segment of the episode, and two of our major collaborations were in the Craft in America Center. Our work together has been featured in numerous magazines and shown in museum exhibits. One of our collaborative works is in the permanent collection of the National Quilt Museum in Paducah, Kentucky.

See if your longarm manufacturer has an ambassador program, and find out how to apply to be one of their brand ambassadors. It's a good mutual arrangement where you can promote their machines and they, in turn, will promote you because they can showcase how you use their machine. Win, win! You may appear in their advertising or other marketing materials, and on their social media accounts. They may invite you to do promotional videos or help with training materials. Just be sure that you are actually gaining something from the arrangement and that the deal is not too one-sided in their favor.

SUBMIT YOUR WORK TO MAGAZINES OR OTHER PUBLICATIONS TO SEE IF YOU CAN GET PUBLISHED. IT'S A WAY TO GET YOUR NAME OUT THERE, GIVING YOU EVEN MORE CREDIBILITY AS A PROFESSIONAL.

Traditional media formats are heavily tied into social media channels these days, so your publicity will not only be through the regular channel, but will most likely be spread to all their social media channels as well. They'll post a link or a clip on Facebook, Tweet about it, or talk about it on Instagram. So, it can spread beyond the original format, and get you a lot of coverage on many platforms. More bang for your buck!

SPEAKING OF THAT... ●▶

SOCIAL MEDIA

If you did your homework from Establish Your Online Presence (page 77), in Chapter 3, then you have already claimed your business's accounts on the most popular social media sites.

THERE ARE A FEW GUIDELINES THAT APPLY NO MATTER WHAT PLATFORM YOU USE:

* Be nice! Operate by the adage, "If you can't say something nice, don't say anything at all."

* Engage often, but be sincere.

* Be encouraging.

* Be humble. No one likes an arrogant braggart.

* Be professional, but approachable.

* Show your work and talk about it.

* If you are going to show client work, be sure you have their permission.

* Post regularly. If someone visits and your most recent post is months old, they'll think you're no longer in business. Keep your account current.

* If someone contacts you, respond in a timely manner.

* And, did I mention? *Be nice.* Always.

Facebook

TO SET UP A FACEBOOK BUSINESS PAGE, IT MUST BE LINKED TO YOUR PERSONAL PROFILE, BUT YOUR PERSONAL PROFILE'S INFORMATION DOES NOT SHOW UP ON YOUR BUSINESS PAGE.

Select a nice profile picture (perhaps your logo?) and cover photo that represent your brand well. For the cover photo, I usually choose a photo of my work and switch it out when I have something new to show. I always use a picture of a quilt that belongs to me, so that I'm not violating a client's rights by posting a photo of a quilt that belongs to them. It can also be misleading if someone thinks I made the quilt and I didn't, even if I am the quilter. A photo of your studio setup or of you hard at work at your machine could work in this spot, too.

You also need a clear, concise written description of your business and services.

Instagram

You can set up a business account on Instagram, but the benefits it provides are more product-oriented than you probably need for a longarm business. A business account does give you the ability to do advertising posts, if that's something you want to do.

If you have a regular Instagram account, you can still do pretty much everything you need to do for your business. Remember to post regularly and have a link to your website in your profile. Use your headshot or your logo, either one, for your profile picture, and try to write a catchy memorable bio or promote your business right in your bio.

YOU CAN SET UP INSTAGRAM TO AUTOMATICALLY CROSS-POST TO FACEBOOK FOR YOU, SO YOU DON'T HAVE TO MANUALLY POST ON BOTH PLATFORMS.

Use hashtags to get your posts seen by more people. It will help you pick up more followers. Use #TBT ("throwback Thursday") and #FBF ("flashback Friday"), to repost some of your older work that new followers may not have seen or even to post something personal that's funny, on Thursdays and Fridays.

Follow hashtags like #longarmquilting or #quilterforhire to see the work of others. Use this hashtag to get your work seen by other quilters, as well.

TAG MANUFACTURERS OF PRODUCTS AND PATTERNS YOU USE WHEN YOU POST. JUST A FEW SUGGESTIONS:

⟶ Maker of the thread and batting

⟶ Designer of the pantograph

⟶ Pattern of the quilt

⟶ Designer and manufacturer of the line of fabric

⟶ Manufacturer of your longarm machine

Those companies may repost your post—or better yet, want to feature you!

Pinterest

I love looking at Pinterest. I'm not so good about posting on Pinterest. My rule for my own Pinterest account, which *is* a business account, is to only post my own photos, so that I'm not accidentally encroaching on someone else's intellectual property. I've created boards for different things I do, and I put my own photos in, which usually link back to my website to a blog post that I've written about the subject, so visitors can find more information if they're interested.

••• You can drive a lot of traffic to your website with Pinterest, so you might create a board for client work and have each photo link back to a blog post you've written about that particular quilt. Remember: If you will be posting photos of client work, make sure you have their permission first.

SET UP BOARDS TO SHOWCASE YOUR BEST WORK, AND MAKE SURE THE LINKS GO BACK TO YOUR WEBSITE SO VISITORS CAN FIND YOU.

Twitter

Just like you can get by on Instagram without a business account, having just a regular account on Twitter is fine. You can set your blog up to automatically post a tweet every time you publish a post. Timing is more important on Twitter than on Facebook or Instagram. Tweets roll in so fast and furious that your current tweet can get buried very quickly, and your audience may never even see it.

TWEET OCCASIONALLY WITH SOME PERTINENT INFORMATION. DON'T GET BOGGED DOWN IN THINKING THAT YOU HAVE TO BE ON IT ALL THE TIME.

YouTube

IF YOU LIKE TO MAKE VIDEOS, YOU CAN START YOUR OWN YOUTUBE CHANNEL. A lot of professional quilters make videos of themselves as they quilt out free-motion designs, give instruction on how to use rulers, demonstrate how to deal with troubling issues that arise with quilts, and all sorts of useful topics. If you have information to share and think it's best done via video, then you might find YouTube a useful medium.

Keep in mind that shooting and editing videos takes time. Make sure you have the time to do it, or build it into your schedule. If you think adding this into your schedule will benefit you, then give it a try. It may not pay off immediately, but if you are looking to expand your business, it might be worth it and pay off down the road.

Integrating Your Platforms

ON ALL THESE PLATFORMS, CROSS-POST AS MUCH AS POSSIBLE. You can set up your blog to automatically Tweet and post to Facebook for you. When you post to your blog, make an Instagram post that tells your followers to visit the blog for more information. If you put up a new YouTube video, post on all the platforms with a link to it.

There are also apps (such as Buffer) that will let you preplan and prewrite your posts and then publish them for you at a specified day and time. If you want to use a post scheduler, do your research or ask your web folks to find out which one might be best for you.

•••• Your web people can tell you (or tell you how to find out) where traffic to your website is coming from. Once you have that information, you can make sure to promote yourself on that space as much as possible.

Your Blog

I call my blog the "home base" of my social media activity. All the social media posting I do is basically either for fun or to get people to visit my blog/website. I post sneak previews, links, snippets, and other brief information and refer them back to my blog for more information. All my social media posts are in real time—I don't use a scheduling app, but I do occasionally prewrite blog posts and schedule them to post at a certain time of day or on a certain date.

HERE ARE SOME TIPS FOR A SUCCESSFUL BLOG:

Don't be absent. If someone asks a question, be sure to answer. Respond to comments on your posts. Be engaged. It shows your readers that you appreciate the fact that they took the time and made the effort to visit, read, and leave a comment.

Be generous with useful information. Host giveaways periodically. Offer discount codes to your subscribers through your newsletter as a reward for being a subscriber and faithful reader.

You don't have to set up a strict schedule for posting, and since you're probably not blogging for a living (you're busy quilting!), an editorial calendar may be overkill, but do try to stay engaged and keep it updated. It takes a long time to craft a blog post, and sometimes your schedule will be too hectic for you to post as often as you'd like, but don't let it slide for too long.

You can prewrite blog posts, and save them as drafts to keep from having to write an entire post all at once. Just chip away at it in a few sessions and eventually you'll have it ready to go. I do this a lot.

When possible, take a little time to visit the blogs of other people, especially if they are readers of your blog, and leave them comments. Be active, but don't let it take over your life. This is how Victoria and I met, so don't count it out!

Keep a list of topics you'd like to write about, and add to it whenever you think of something. Then, if you're ever stuck for a topic, you can choose something from the list.

Potential customers will be studying the type of work you do and will want to see samples and photos or want to know what pantograph or computerized designs you can do, so be sure to post about these things.

Be sure to include some personal stuff now and then, so people can get to know you a little better.

Injecting some of your personality into your blog makes it unique, and sharing some personal stories can keep your blog from sounding stiff and stuffy. I can't help it, I write like I talk (this book is a good case in point!), and I post about my goats all the time. My boy Ranger (#rangerthegoat) has his own little fan club!

Be real—don't always show only the pretty. I post periodic photos of the state of my cutting table. It's always a disaster, and I don't have the Instagram-worthy perfect studio shots to post. I know there are others like me, so it's good to help them feel they're not alone.

I recommend doing even more research about marketing—that topic could be an entire book by itself, and I'm not the one to write it! There is a wealth of information out there.

CHAPTER 8

expanding

AS YOUR BUSINESS GROWS, YOU MAY DECIDE THERE ARE OTHER THINGS YOU CAN DO TO MAKE THINGS EVEN MORE PROFITABLE FOR YOUR BUSINESS. You may have so much work coming in that it makes sense to add more equipment and hire some help. You may want to teach or add some other forms of income. If that is the case, read on....

ADDING MORE EQUIPMENT

By this, I mainly mean: Get a second longarm machine. And it should probably be computerized. Many professional quilters for hire own two longarm machines: one computerized and another that may or may not be computerized. While the computerized machine is stitching out its computerized designs, the quilter is manually running the other machine to do custom or free-motion work, allowing them to turn out many more quilts in less time.

I also know a few quilters for hire who own embroidery machines. If you do, you can offer custom embroidery designs, such as embroidering labels for customers' quilts, putting designs on blocks for them, or even applying designs to hats and clothing for customers who aren't quiltmakers. While the embroidery machine is stitching away, you can be running the longarm and quilting quilts.

HIRING HELP

If you get to the point where you want to take on more work, but it's simply not possible because you can't spread yourself any thinner, it may be time to think about hiring help.

Select candidates carefully, make sure they know their job description, and provide them with all the proper training.

You can hire an assistant to take over some of the hats you're currently wearing. This can lighten your load, letting you take on more quilting jobs.

HIRING OUT YOUR BOOKKEEPING AND ACCOUNTING AND HIRING WEB DEVELOPERS TO TAKE CARE OF THE BACKGROUND PARTS OF YOUR WEBSITE ARE THINGS YOU COULD GET OFF YOUR PLATE AND WILL ALLEVIATE A LOT OF STRESS. This is money well spent if you're trying to free up some time and make your life easier.

••• You will still spend time doing paperwork and updating your website—but hiring help to take care of the hard parts takes a lot of the worry off your shoulders. And believe me, when a real problem arises, it's nice to be able to call them and just let them deal with it, while you keep right on working.

An office assistant can help with administrative tasks: managing inventory, placing supply orders, paying bills, handling correspondence and email, keeping the studio clean and organized, helping with marketing and social media, running errands, and shipping/ delivering finished quilts. Look over your Time Log (page 111) and see if there are chunks of time that would be freed up if you had someone else helping you.

If you hire employees, you have to apply for an EIN (Employer Identification Number) and make sure to follow all the rules for paying taxes related to having employees. Review your finances to make sure you can afford to pay an employee and to determine whether having an employee will allow you to make more income and not simply end up costing you more money.

If you hire help, and you intend to have them help you with the actual longarm quilting (which I *don't* recommend), make sure that you disclose this information to your customers.

Your customers bring you their quilts because they like *your* work, and they expect to get *your* work on their quilt. If you let your employee do the work for you (even if it's computerized), it's not *your* work, and it's not what your client is expecting. You *must* disclose this information ahead of time, and make sure your clients are okay with it *before* you do it.

My advice: Do your own quilting and let your employees help you in supporting roles.

TEACHING OTHERS

Once you've gained enough experience, you may want to teach what you know to others. This can be done in a variety of ways. The simplest is to publish tutorials right on your own blog or to post videos on your YouTube channel. But these don't necessarily get you any money.

Teaching Hands-on Classes

FOR ONE-ON-ONE PRIVATE CLASSES, YOU CAN DO THIS RIGHT IN YOUR OWN STUDIO, WHERE YOU HAVE EVERYTHING YOU NEED RIGHT AT YOUR FINGERTIPS. Set up appointments, establish your pricing, and host students in your studio for a day of learning. This way, you can tailor your one-on-one class to each particular student, enabling them to learn the things they feel they need the most help with, and they'll have you all to themselves for all the questions they want to ask. If you have two machines, you could have two students at a time and make even more money. Make sure your insurance covers having clients in your home for this purpose.

Teaching at Quilt Shops

If a shop has a longarm machine, they may want to pay you to teach their customers how to use the machine so they can rent it out. They may want you to train an employee to use their machine so they can do quilting for customers. Don't worry that this is going to hurt your business too much—if you're doing well enough that you're looking to expand in this way, it can only be a good thing. It'll give you one more place to refer your overflow to, as well!

Teaching at Quilt Shows That Offer Longarm Classes

Some of these classes can be hands-on with actual longarm machines provided at the show. Some may be theory only, where students learn design or other techniques that may not require them to be at a machine. Check the class schedules at major shows and see if they offer these types of classes. Think about what you have to offer that isn't currently being taught. Put together a pro-posal for what you'd like to teach, then find out how you can apply to be an instructor at one of these shows. Most major shows have a website, and the application for applying to be an instructor can be found there.

Teaching Online Classes

There are a lot of platforms for offering online classes, so do your research. Some require you to do all the work (filming, editing, post-ing, selling, support,…) yourself, some help you with that, and others do most of that for you. Different platforms pay differently: Some let you keep some of the profits; some only pay you royalties. I've included some starting points in Resources (page 205).

Teaching for Guilds or Groups

This usually involves having a venue with a longarm machine set up and that is large enough to handle a group of people. You present and demonstrate, and a few of the students can have a bit of hands-on time. Group size should be limited so that everyone will be able to see the demonstrations while gathered around the machine.

Trunk Shows

You can offer trunk shows of your work to groups or guilds. This gives you the opportunity to show a lot of examples of your work and talk about them and how they were done. Attendees can get a closer look and ask you questions once your show-and-tell is over. Hand out business cards and brochures in case any of the attendees want to become customers.

Writing a Book

If you've developed a technique that you think can be taught through a book, consider submitting a proposal to a publisher. Look at all the books on longarm quilting currently available, and see if you have anything different to offer. Book publishers usually have their pro-posal guidelines on their website.

Writing for Magazines

You can submit articles on machine-quilting topics to magazines. Check the magazine's website for their submission guidelines. Some will even state what types of articles they are looking for.

RENTING TIME

If you have more than one longarm machine, or a light schedule, you may want to consider renting out your machine to those who want to quilt their own quilts but who don't own their own longarm machine. Don't let this turn into a full-on teaching session, however. That's an entirely different thing!

••• To rent your longarm, you usually charge by the hour. Your clients will probably need a way to remove quilts from the machine and easily load them back on for the next session, such as zippered leaders or Renae's Red Snappers (see Designing Patterns and Tools, below), if they don't finish before their time is up.

Since you don't want them destroying your expensive machine, it's wise to require them to take a class to learn how the machine operates before you turn them loose on it. And you will need good insurance! Not only on your machine, but also to cover having clients in your studio.

DESIGNING PATTERNS AND TOOLS

IN ALL YOUR PRACTICING, WORKING, AND GAINING EXPERIENCE OVER TIME, YOU MAY EVENTUALLY COME UP WITH YOUR OWN VERSION OF THE PERFECT TOOL TO MAKE DOING CERTAIN TASKS EASIER. A lot of quilters have designed tools that work with longarm machines to make things faster and easier; for example, quilter Renae Haddadin, of Quilts on the Corner, designed Renae's Red Snappers to make loading a quilt on the frame easier.

Even more quilters have designed rulers for specific purposes: sets of curves, angles, and shapes that make doing custom work easier. I've listed a few in Resources (page 205).

If you think you have a good idea for a product that will make long-arm quilting easier for yourself and others, do your research on how to get it developed into a product that you can sell. You can even plan some of your classes around your own tools.

••• You can also design pantograph patterns or designs for blocks, borders, sashing, and more, which can be digitized and sold to quilters with computerized machines. Quilters for hire are always looking to increase their library of designs, as it gives them more choices to offer their clients. If you're good at coming up with new designs, consider offering them to other quilters for hire to make some extra money. You can even create paper pantograph patterns in a format that can be sold digitally and printed by the purchaser themselves.

Attending Quilt Market, the semiannual trade show for the quilting industry, will help you make a lot of connections with people who can assist you with your plans to expand. Quilt Market is attended by companies who can help you develop new tools, get your designs published and into the hands of customers, help you with marketing materials, or assist you in developing your online classes.

PART 2

PIECING AND CUSTOM QUILTMAKING FOR HIRE

While the first part of this book is all about quilting tops for other people, this part addresses making complete quilts, start to finish, for hire. Whether you make quilts for sale or you work on commission when someone hires you to make a quilt especially for them, there are a few extra things to take into consideration.

The bulk of the information presented in Part 1 applies to you in this case, so be sure to work your way through Part 1 first—I won't be repeating any of that here. Once you've done that, read the chapters in Part 2. This is where I'll be talking about additional things you need to be aware of.

CHAPTER 9

getting started

IF YOU'RE ALREADY A QUILTMAKER AND YOU'VE BEEN MAKING QUILTS FOR FAMILY AND FRIENDS FOR A WHILE, maybe you're ready to take things up a notch and start creating them for other people, too.

If you're a longarm quilter who quilts for hire and you're looking to add custom quiltmaking into your lineup of offerings, great! It can add another source of income and some welcome variety into your day-to-day business. However, you will need to stay very organized and schedule carefully.

FINDING YOUR NICHE

> "Seriously, is it 'nitch'? Or 'nish'? Or 'neesh'? Does anyone really know?" ~ AUTHOR

The best way to find your niche is not to look outward at a specific demographic or one particular type of customer, but to look inward and ask, "What problem can I solve for my clients?" or "What problem do I want to solve for my clients?"

YOU CAN'T BE ALL THINGS TO ALL PEOPLE, AND YOU ARE JUST ONE PERSON, SO YOU CAN'T DO EVERYTHING. Sorry, but it's simply not possible. The best thing might be for you to specialize in a certain type of quilt that you enjoy making, yet can still make a profit from. *Remember:* If you're not making a profit, then it's not a business, it's just a hobby... and likely an expensive one!

Some quilters make memory quilts for their clients using clothing from loved ones, baby clothes, special T-shirts, and other sentimental fabrics. This type of quilt cuts down on your expenses for materials, since most of the materials are being supplied by the client and your job is to incorporate them into a finished creation. It also reduces the quilt-making costs for the client, since they're providing the bulk of the materials for the quilt top.

8: GETTING STARTED

SOME QUILTERS MAKE A CERTAIN TYPE OF QUILT GEARED TO A CERTAIN AUDIENCE. For example, quilts using fabrics from their clients' favorite sports teams, or quilts with a theme like camping, hunting or fishing, golf, cartoon characters, and more... and have you seen the ones made from Crown Royal bags? As a quilter for hire, you might be surprised at some of the jobs you get asked to tackle!

Some quilters make samples—for quilt shops, for fabric companies, or for designers. These clients all know that samples help sell patterns and fabric. Quilt shops need samples made year-round to promote their products. Fabric companies and designers usually need samples made for the semiannual trade show, Quilt Market. They have a short window of time to get the samples made, so they need help. If you can turn out quality work in a short time span, you could be the help they need!

> If a client contacts you with a specific request that doesn't work for you, don't be afraid to decline the job. If you think it doesn't fit with the type of quilts you make, or you can't do their request justice, or it might not be profitable for you, just say no.

If someone requests something you've been wanting to try anyway, that's great! Go for it. It'll give you a chance to try it and make money at the same time.

DO YOUR RESEARCH

FIND OUT WHO YOUR COMPETITION IS.

* Where do their customers come from?

* What can you do that is different from what they do?

* If you will be doing the same thing or something very similar, where will your customers come from?

* Will you bring in clients from a wider area by marketing your services online rather than just locally?

Finding customers who want a quilt made completely from scratch on commission is slightly more difficult than finding customers who simply want the tops they've made to be quilted. Finding customers who want to pay you what your work is worth is even more difficult.

You may not make a living doing solely commission work, but it can be a good supplement to your other income. Having multiple sources of revenue is never a bad idea.

Angela Steiner, of Angela's Heirloom Quilting, makes quilts for her clients out of their baby's clothing. She works on these in between longarm quilting projects for her regular clients. This gives her extra work, so that the slow times don't hurt her income.

Melanie Miller-Thurnau, of Sew & 'Taylor' Too, makes T-shirt quilts for her clients and also has a booming business doing alterations of all types, especially for weddings and proms.

IF YOU SIMPLY WANT TO MAKE QUILTS FOR SALE, RESEARCH THE POPULAR TRENDS TO SEE WHAT TYPES OF QUILTS ARE SELLING. Browse Etsy shops and see what's out there. Young couples having babies usually want something modern-looking in the current popular nursery colors. People shopping for wedding gifts might be looking for something in a particular decorating theme, such as farmhouse, mid-century modern, or lake living. Someone may see something you've made and request a custom quilt made similar simply because they saw your ready-made one.

DEVELOP YOUR PRODUCT

It's All About Quality

There are a lot of people and companies in the world selling quilts. Many of them don't charge enough money for those quilts to even cover the cost of the materials they have in them, let alone make a profit. So how do you make quilts, charge what they're worth, and be able to sell them and make a profit? How do you compete with the big chain stores selling king-size quilts for $48?

• • • • ▶ TWO WORDS: QUALITY WORKMANSHIP.

Develop a superior, high-quality, unique, handmade product that you can be proud of, and don't even flinch if someone tells you your prices are too high. Because they aren't. We'll discuss pricing in Chapter 11, but I'm mentioning it here so that you're not put off from the start about whether you should even do this.

You should always use the highest-quality materials in your creations; do your best, most careful stitching; and create a quality item that your client will treasure for years to come. Even if they're buying it to be a "usin' quilt," you will have made sure that it will hold up to years of loving usin'! Haven't you? (Yes, you have!)

Originality and Asking Permission

WHEN YOU MAKE A QUILT FOR SALE, MAKE SURE THAT IT IS AN ORIGINAL DESIGN OF YOUR OWN. If it is not, you must check with the original designer and ask permission to create a quilt (or multiple quilts) from their pattern that you will be making a profit from. It is illegal to profit from the work of someone else, and most pattern designers prohibit the use of their patterns for anything other than personal use, unless you ask and receive explicit permission.

••• If a client asks you to make a quilt for them from a specific pattern, you still need to check with the pattern designer to make sure that it's all right with them if you do this. If a fabric company asks you to make a quilt for them from a specific pattern, be sure to ask them if they have been granted the proper permission from the designer.

Don't think of this as a huge hurdle. It's not a difficult thing to do. Most of the time, the designer's contact information is located somewhere on the pattern, so you can simply drop them a kind email, let them know what you're wanting to do, and see if they will grant you permission.

When they reply, you will have your answer in writing. If it's a no, let your client know, and choose a different pattern. If the answer is yes, print out a copy of that email and keep it with the rest of the paperwork for the quilt.

Remember also that creating a design of a copyrighted or trade-marked item is illegal, such as making a quilt with a company's logo, band's logo, or sports team's insignia, or even a certain cartoon character. You can use fabric with those things on them, because the fabric manufacturer has been given the rights to create the fabric for sale, but you cannot create the design of the logo or character out of your own fabric. If you're unsure if what you want to make is legal, consult with a lawyer who understands copyright and trademark laws before you begin.

Do these things because your reputation is at stake. You want to keep your good reputation so you can stay in business.

SPREAD THE WORD

IF YOU ALREADY HAVE A WEBSITE AND SOCIAL MEDIA ACCOUNTS, MAKE SURE THERE IS INFORMATION IN ALL THOSE PLACES ABOUT THE FACT THAT YOU QUILT ON COMMISSION OR THAT YOU HAVE QUILTS FOR SALE.

You can sell ready-made quilts directly through Facebook and Instagram, or on your blog, simply by posting there and telling buyers how to order and pay.

You could have a page on your website showing the ready-made quilts you have for sale with information about how they can be purchased. If you have an Etsy shop, you can refer them there, or if you find it's worth the extra money, you could have an online shop added directly to your website. Your web people can help you with this, and help you decide if that is something you want to do.

You should also add a page to your website outlining how a client would go about contacting you and working with you to create a quilt on commission. Post answers to a few commonly asked questions, give them some initial information, and offer a way to easily contact you to start the process of designing a quilt just for them.

••• Showing your commission work at a guild meeting won't help grow your business—those people already know how to make their own quilts. You're preaching to the choir there! Commission jobs usually come from people who don't know how to create their own custom quilts. However, attending a trade show to talk to fabric companies and designers about making samples for them might prove lucrative.

Ask at your local quilt shops to see if they need someone to make samples for them. If they need help, you can work out the details of patterns, fabrics, quilting, and so on, with them. If it's something you want to do and their terms are satisfactory to you, go ahead and take the job.

NOTES

_____

_____

_____

_____

_____

_____

_____

_____

_____

CHAPTER 10

getting set up

WHETHER YOU ARE A QUILT PIECER AND A QUILTER, or just one or the other, you need to consider your physical space and how you will do what you do. Here are some ideas to consider.

EQUIPMENT AND TOOLS

Longarm or Not?

You don't necessarily have to have a longarm machine to make custom quilts for sale. My friend, Melanie Miller-Thurnau, of Sew & 'Taylor' Too, makes T-shirt memory quilts for her clients but does not own a longarm machine. She stays busy year-round, with some rush periods around graduation time; in late summer, when students take off for college; and at Christmas.

She and her sewing team create the tops from shirts her clients provide, along with some additional fabrics she uses in the tops. She hires the quilting part out to longarmers like me and simply builds that cost into her price for the finished quilt. She is able to make more quilts this way, since she hires out a big chunk of the labor.

My bestie, Victoria Findlay Wolfe, does high-end custom commissions for clients who seek her out. She, too, designs and makes the tops, then sends them to me for the quilting part. She also builds my charges into her price for the finished quilt.

Karen McTavish, of McTavish Quilting Studio, does the opposite! She accepts commission work through her studio and hires out the piecing part. Once the top is completed by one of her contracted piecers, she quilts and binds the quilt, building all the charges incurred into her final price.

••• So, if you don't want to invest in a longarm machine or if longarming is a skill you don't have and don't want to develop, you don't have to—and the same goes if you're so busy with the longarm that it makes more sense for you to hire out the piecing. Hire that part out, and price your work accordingly.

Sewing Machine

If you will be piecing tops for clients (whether or not you do the quilting part yourself), you need a good workhorse of a sewing machine. There are more brands and types of sewing machines than you can shake a stick at. If you're reading this book, you most likely already have at least one sewing machine.

IF YOU'RE IN THE MARKET FOR A GOOD MACHINE, DO YOUR RESEARCH TO MAKE SURE THE ONE YOU GET WILL BE ABLE TO DO EVERYTHING YOU WANT IT TO DO.

✳ Will you need anything more than a straight stitch?

✳ Do you need a zigzag stitch or other specialty or decorative stitches?

✳ Will you need special feet to do things like piping, buttonholes, zippers, or ruffles?

✳ What regular features (such as a thread cutter, needle threader, ...) would you like to have included on your machine?

✳ What kind of support and training will you get with the model you select?

Shop around and test-drive different machines. Talk to dealers and ask them questions about the features of each machine. Narrow it down to your favorites, and then choose the one that you think will be best for you. It's probably *the* most important tool for your business, so choose wisely, and don't settle for something inferior just to save money.

Sewing Supplies

You also need the regular sewing supplies (just to name a few!):

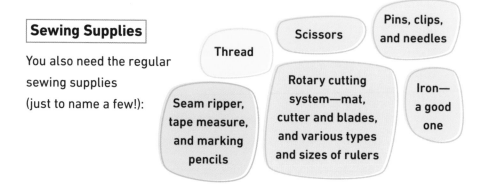

Thread

Scissors

Pins, clips, and needles

Seam ripper, tape measure, and marking pencils

Rotary cutting system—mat, cutter and blades, and various types and sizes of rulers

Iron— a good one

You probably already have most of these. Some need to be replenished or replaced periodically as they get used up or worn out. Remember to build these things into your budget.

Fabric and Batting

You will also need fabric and batting on hand. For most quilters, having a fabric stash is not a problem at all! You can probably make many, many quilts for sale simply by shopping at home.

For commission quilts, you will be working with the customer and probably buying fabric specific to their requests, so keep a budget set aside to use for purchasing fabric.

ORGANIZING YOUR SPACE

YOU WILL NEED A CONVENIENT WORKSPACE TO SET UP, AT THE VERY LEAST:

* Table for cutting, planning, and laying things out

* Sewing machine station with room to work and keep your necessary tools at hand

* Ironing station

If you have a wall in your sewing area that you can dedicate to using as a design wall, it will be an added bonus, and you will find it invaluable in helping you lay out your designs.

You will also need storage for the things you're not using all the time, such as your thread collection, fabric, tools and notions, and other items.

It's also important to have a good storage solution for any works-in-progress. This could be stackable storage bins, a rolling cart with drawers, or a closet or cupboard with appropriate shelving.

If you have a computerized longarm machine, it would be ideal to have your sewing area in the same space as your longarm machine, or at least really close. Then, while the computer is running the longarm, you can be working on your commission job, essentially doubling your work time. If it's not computerized, this doesn't matter as much.

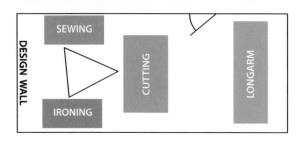

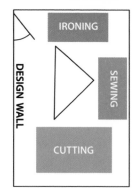

The ideal setup for your three main work surfaces is a triangle configuration, so you can easily move between the stations to do your work. This increases productivity by having everything together in the most logical way.

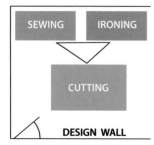

If you have pets, be sure to alert your customers to this fact. Even if the pets have not touched the quilt, if *you* touch your pet and then touch the quilt, it can transfer. In case someone is severely allergic, they need to be warned.

I have a dog and some cats, but they are not allowed into the studio if I have anything out and within their reach that belongs to a customer. If I'm only working on my own things, they can come in briefly with strict supervision (usually weekends). Otherwise, I have doors that keep them out. But every time I go downstairs, I invariably pet or hold one of them, so that could possibly transfer allergens without me even thinking about it. Because of this, I do not advertise my studio as being pet-free, even though the pets are not generally in close proximity to customer items.

If you're a smoker, or live with a smoker, you *must* also alert your customers, as well. Some people are super-sensitive to the cigarette smoke smell, and if they are nonsmokers, the odor might be offensive to them.

If your home is smoke-free and pet-free, however, feel free to advertise that.

Plan Your Studio Layout

To plan your setup, you can use a piece of graph paper. Measure your studio space, and mark the outline on your graph paper, using one square to equal 1 foot (12 inches), or some other increment that makes sense to you. Mark the outline with any windows, doors, closets, or other permanent fixtures that you might need to work around.

Then consider each piece of furniture or equipment you will have in the room. Measure each one of these. On a separate piece of graph paper, mark the outlines of each of these pieces, and cut them out. In addition to your three main workstations, don't forget any storage pieces you might have, such as cabinets, rolling carts, or small tables. If your long-arm machine is included in your plan, make sure you take into account the working area *around* the machine you will need.

••• Now, arrange all your furniture pieces on your room layout graph to see how they will all fit. You can keep rearranging until you have your perfect setup. Then you can arrange the actual pieces in the room to match your graph-paper layout.

One huge benefit of planning it out like this is to prevent you from having to move all the furniture over and over again. You plan it out on paper before you ever lift a finger, then only move the pieces once.

"Work smart, not hard!" ~ MY COWBOY

Use the following graph paper pages to get you started. You can copy it or play right in these pages. Measure and mark the outline of your studio on the graph paper, then (using a different sheet of paper that's not from this book!) make some cutouts of your furniture pieces so you can play around with their arrangement.

ADDING QUILTMAKING TO YOUR SCHEDULE

As hard as I've found it to schedule just the longarming part of my business, it's even more difficult to plan how long a commission quilt might take and fit that in along with all the regularly scheduled work.

> "Is this gonna be one o' those times where I hafta drive you somewhere while yer whippin' down a binding?"
>
> ~ MY COWBOY

Read the information presented in Scheduling (page 107) and Organizing Your Time (page 111) and try to brainstorm some ideas of when you can fit custom quiltmaking into your schedule. Use your Time Log to see if you need to do any rearranging of your weekly schedule to make time for this extra work.

⟶ Is there something you need to quit doing (even temporarily)?

⟶ Are there things that you can delegate or hire out that would not cut into your profits too much?

⟶ Or are you able to fit this type of work into gaps you already have in your schedule?

WHEN I HAVE A COMMISSION QUILT TO WORK ON, I TRY TO WORK ON IT IN THE MORNINGS AND THEN RUN THE LONGARM IN THE AFTERNOONS. I take on only two to three commissions per year, so once the commission is done, I can add other work back into those spots in my schedule. If you're hiring out the quilting part, you may have room in your schedule to take on extra commission jobs.

••• Keep your client's deadline in mind and use backward planning to figure out how much you need to accomplish each day or week in order to get the job done in time. Be sure to build in time for a few interruptions and unexpected delays along the way. If you're traveling or taking a vacation, don't forget to take that into account.

IF YOU DO A LOT OF COMMISSION WORK IN ADDITION TO LONGARMING FOR CUSTOMERS, THEN YOU CAN SIMPLY BUILD TIME FOR THE COMMISSION QUILTS INTO YOUR WEEKLY SCHEDULE AND SCHEDULE YOUR LONGARMING JOBS ACCORDINGLY. Don't forget to schedule the quilting of the commission quilts into your longarm schedule!

If you're creating only the tops and hiring the longarming out, then you need to work closely with your longarm quilter to make sure they can help you meet the deadlines you have for your clients. This may mean reserving spots on their schedule well in advance and having your part done early in order to give them enough time to do their part. Don't forget, you'll probably have some finishing touches to add when you get it back, too, such as adding the label and doing the binding. And remember to build in shipping time if you have to ship the quilt to the client. You don't want to have to ask and pay for a rush fee!

CHAPTER 11

money, contracts, and help—oh my!

CUSTOM QUILTMAKING FOR HIRE INVOLVES A LOT MORE DETAILS THAN SIMPLY QUILTING A TOP SOMEONE ELSE HAS ALREADY MADE. So. Many. More. Details. We'll go over all that, so you don't forget something important as you negotiate for a commission job.

THE QUILTMAKING AGREEMENT

Reaching agreement with a client on an entire quilt is much more difficult than simply deciding what quilting designs to add to their finished quilt top. They may have a grand idea in their head about what they want, or they may have no idea at all. They may have a great idea but not know how to articulate it. They may have dreamed up the absolutely impossible because they aren't aware of all that the quiltmaking process entails.

But this is why they have come to you in the first place: Most of your clients will be people who don't have the skills to do this for themselves, and some of them will not understand the skill, time, and expense involved. It's your job to come up with a plan that you can agree on for a finished product that they will love and to make it in a price range that they are comfortable with, all while making sure that you are earning a proper profit from the job.

MAKE YOURSELF A QUESTIONNAIRE THAT COVERS ALL THE INITIAL QUESTIONS YOU AND YOUR CLIENT WILL HAVE FOR EACH OTHER. INCLUDE AT LEAST THE FOLLOWING QUESTIONS, AND ADD MORE AS YOU THINK OF THEM:

* Do they have a specific deadline they need the quilt by?

* What size does the quilt need to be?

* What colors do they want their quilt to be?

* What colors do they like or dislike?

* Do they have a design in mind?

* Who is the quilt for? (Baby, college student, newlyweds, retiree? What gender?)

* Will the quilt be made with T-shirts or clothing?

* Is there a specific theme involved?

* What type of machine quilting design do they want the top to be finished with?

If you're sewing samples for a shop, fabric company, or designer, they will provide you with all the details, materials, and pattern they'd like you to use, which takes most of the guesswork out of the job. You will probably supply thread and sometimes batting, but these jobs make providing a quote and doing the work a lot easier than coming up with something from scratch for an individual commission.

COMMISSION WORK PRICES

> *"I was watching the movie Monte Walsh with My Cowboy. When Martine says to Monte, 'I operate in a profession of diminishing returns,' My Cowboy snorted, 'Ha! She must be a quilter!'"* ~ AUTHOR

PRICING COMMISSION WORK IS A TEETH-GNASHING SUBJECT FOR MANY QUILTERS. We have all been conditioned to be filled with doubt when quoting a price for our finished products, even though we know the amount of blood, sweat, tears, time, and money we've put into it.

But I'm here to tell you: Don't back down.

Don't let someone tell you you're charging too much.
Don't let that make you feel bad or doubt yourself.

If someone is asking you to make a quilt for them, they are asking you—*a skilled quilter*—who has made a huge investment in your business, to apply that skill and use your equipment to create for them a personalized quality product that will last for years and hold special memories for them. If they were able and willing to do it themselves, don't you think they would?

They are seeking you out because they *don't* have those skills, and they should not be expecting to get *your* skills for cheap. Your job is to kindly educate them on everything that is involved in making them the custom product they want.

YOU WILL UNDOUBTEDLY COME INTO CONTACT WITH A PROSPECTIVE CUS-TOMER WHO WILL LOOK DOWN THEIR NOSE AT YOUR QUOTE, AND SAY, "WELL! SO-AND-SO SAID THEY WOULD DO IT FOR (X AMOUNT)." And there *are* plenty of quilters out there who are underpricing their work. These quilters are most likely not trying to make a living wage from a business. They are simply doing a few commissions on the side now and then, and taking whatever amount they feel they can get, a lot of times as a favor to a friend.

When you hear this, you simply have to tell them, "That's a great bargain price! I can't even source the materials for that amount. I think you should get so-and-so to do it for you." You cannot afford to cheat yourself and end up basically paying the client to take the quilt from you after you've made it, because that's what it will boil down to.

You also cannot afford to do it simply for "what it costs you in materials" and not charge for your labor or overhead costs. You'll still be losing money. If you're in business for real, you could have spent that same amount of time doing something that would have made you money. Not charging for your labor and overhead is just wasting time you will never get back, and thus costing you money.

Keeping an itemized accounting of the expenses incurred in making the quilt will help you explain it to your client, both in the estimate ahead of time, and at final invoice time.

Many things factor into the pricing of a custom quiltmaking job. Let's get started.

Overhead

The meter is always running on overhead costs, whether you're being productive or not. The money to pay these bills has to come from somewhere, and you need to be making enough money to pay them. So, building overhead costs into your prices is not unacceptable at all.

YOU CAN CALCULATE HOW TO ADD THESE INTO YOUR PRICING BY CALCULATING YOUR AVERAGE MONTHLY EXPENSES FOR THINGS SUCH AS:

* Equipment upkeep and maintenance

* Utilities: electricity, phone/internet, water, trash service

* Website maintenance and fees

* Bookkeeping, accounting, and bank fees

* Supplies and tools (but *not* purchases of materials and inventory)

* Studio lease or rent and maintenance (if applicable)

* Contingencies, such as unexpected business expenses and repairs

* Business loan payment

* Insurance

* Taxes

If some of these are only yearly or quarterly expenses, divide them up to figure out the monthly fee. For example, if you pay your insurance quarterly, divide the amount you pay by 3 to arrive at the monthly amount.

If your utilities bills are for your entire house, and not just your studio, you can take a percentage of the entire bill as the cost for your studio space. For example, my studio is one-third of my house, so I would divide my utility bills by 3, and use that amount for my overhead calculations. If your utilities vary a lot over the course of a year, you could total up a year's worth of bills, then divide by 12, to get an average for one month, then divide it by the percentage you use for your studio.

Once you know your monthly expenses, divide that number by the number of hours you work in a month. The resulting total is how much your overhead expenses are costing you per hour.

WANNA DO A RUN-THROUGH OF AN EXAMPLE? LET'S DO IT. I'M USING EASY HYPO-
THETICAL NUMBERS TO MAKE THE MATH EASIER, BUT THIS WILL GIVE YOU AN
IDEA OF HOW TO FIGURE THIS INTO YOUR PRICING.

QUILTING FOR HIRE

Monthly overhead expenses	Example numbers	Your numbers
Equipment upkeep and maintenance	$30	_____
Utilities: electricity, phone/ internet, water, trash service	$145	_____
Website maintenance and fees	$90	_____
Bookkeeping, accounting, and bank fees	$75	_____
Supplies and tools (but not purchases of materials and inventory)	$20	_____
Studio lease or rent and maintenance (if applicable)	—	_____
Contingencies, such as unexpected business expenses and repairs	$50	_____
Business loan payment (if applicable)	—	_____
Insurance	$25	_____
Taxes	$90	_____
Total monthly overhead expenses	**$525**	_____
How many hours per month do you work?	175 hours	_____
Total hourly overhead expenses (monthly overhead expenses divided by hours worked per month)	**$3 per hour**	_____

Hypothetically speaking, you can see that $3 of every hour of my labor goes toward paying my monthly overhead expenses. Fill in your own real numbers in the blank column of the chart to figure out how much of your hourly labor rate goes to pay your monthly overhead expenses.

••• Your expenses (and possibly the number of hours you work) may vary from month to month, so you may want to redo your numbers every few months to make sure you're still charging enough, especially if you've added in any new expense categories.

Right away, you can see that in order to not *lose* money on a job, I would automatically need to charge at least $3 per hour for labor. (That doesn't include making any profit.)

Materials

MATERIALS INCLUDE FABRIC, BATTING, THREAD, NOTIONS, AND ANY OTHER SUPPLIES YOU PUT INTO THE CREATION OF THE QUILT. Also consider other items besides quilts that you might make. For instance, if you make a matching pillow, you would have a pillow form or stuffing and possibly a zipper or buttons, to add into the equation. If the quilt is embellished, you will have the cost of those embellishments to include.

Keep careful records of the purchases of materials you make for any particular job. I usually keep all receipts and invoices for a particular job together with the rest of the paperwork. You can put everything in an envelope or folder and keep it with the job from start to finish; this way, all the paperwork is together, making it much easier for you to complete the invoice later.

If you use materials from your stash that you did not purchase specifically for the job, keep track of what they are, and how much of them you used, including how much yardage you use, so you can include that in your pricing.

••• You should charge full price for these materials—don't cheat yourself! Even if you think it should be discounted because you "already had it laying around," you'll likely have to pay full price to replenish these materials.

However, if you know you bought it on sale, and remember what you paid for it, you can choose to charge accordingly. When you go to replenish it, you might once again find a good bargain and not have to pay full price! The choice is yours.

> *"Since it is my business, I get to determine when and how much I can be benevolent."* ~ **MELANIE MILLER-THURNAU, OF SEW & 'TAYLOR' TOO** ✳

For thread, you can charge a per-bobbin price or simply estimate how much of a spool or cone you used, and prorate the charge based on the cost of the full spool.

Labor

Here's the big one. The one where we usually try to justify cheating ourselves out of well-deserved money.

"How much do you think your hourly rate should be? $10? $20? $30? You are certainly worth more than minimum wage. You are a skilled craftsperson. In my case, I've been quilting for 25 years and sewing for 43. This is not an insignificant statement. If you hire that depth of skill to lay tile in your house or make cabinets for your kitchen, it will cost you more than $20 an hour. My years of skill ensures the quilt is well constructed, made of quality materials (chosen with a discerning eye and years of practice), and executed with knowledge and a passion for the artistry and craft. This is worth a lot." ~ **SAM HUNTER, HUNTER'S DESIGN STUDIO***

* Sam has an entire series of articles on her website (huntersdesignstudio.com) that covers this topic called "We Are $ew Worth It."

MELANIE MILLER-THURNAU, OF SEW & 'TAYLOR' TOO, BASES HER LABOR COST ON FOUR BASIC CONCEPTS:

* **What education and background have I acquired to make me the skilled person I am today?**

* **Can anyone else perform my skill?**

* **Is my charge appropriate for the social culture I'm living in?**

* **Is it fair?**

You already know from figuring out your monthly overhead expenses that you need to charge at least a minimum hourly rate to cover your operating expenses. You then need to add to that the hourly wage you think you should be making. You should definitely not be working for less than minimum wage, and since you are performing tasks that require special skills, you really deserve more than minimum wage.

IT'S ENTIRELY ACCEPTABLE TO HAVE ONE WAGE RATE THAT YOU CHARGE FOR A JOB THAT WILL BE SIMPLE TO DO, AND ANOTHER HIGHER WAGE RATE FOR A JOB THAT WILL REQUIRE MORE SKILL.

Once you've arrived at the hourly amount you will be charging for your skilled labor, it's time to itemize out the labor you're doing for a particular job.

Did you spend three hours drafting up a custom design, discussing it with the customer, revising it till it was approved, and then figuring out the amount of materials the design will need? You get to charge for that.

You also get to charge for the time you spend cutting, piecing, quilting, and finishing, including any time spent doing handwork, such as adding embellishments, doing appliqué, sewing on buttons, or whipping down binding.

Keep careful records of the time you spend on every step of the creation process. It's difficult to remember to keep track of your time, especially once you get engrossed in your work, so you have to be diligent about not cheating yourself.

THERE ARE SEVERAL WAYS YOU CAN DO THIS:

→ There are apps you can download for your phone, tablet, or computer that help you track the time you spend. Some of them have more features than others, and let you track multiple jobs and sort the time into various categories. Some of them simply work like a time clock: Clock in, clock out. Do your research and see if there's one you'd like to try.

→ You can log the time manually on a sheet of paper you keep with your notes for the job.

→ You can log your time in a computer spreadsheet program, such as Microsoft Excel or Apple Numbers.

→ You can use a chalkboard or whiteboard in your studio.

Now that you have all the ingredients, you'll be able to easily whip up your quote, contract, and the final invoice!

PAPERWORK/CONTRACTS

While I stated in Paperwork (page 88), in Chapter 4, that I don't believe you need a formal contract for longarming service, doing a quilt on commission is a horse of a different color. While you are reaching agreement on what exactly you will be doing for the client and what exactly they want you to do for them, there will be a *lot* of back-and-forth communication. Keep good notes, and save all emails related to the job.

The first thing you need to know is if they need this quilt for an event with a specific deadline, such as a graduation, wedding, or other important event. Some nonquilters have no idea of the time it takes to make a quilt, so they may not give you enough notice. If you cannot fit the job into your schedule and meet their deadline, no further discussion is necessary.

> Be sure *not* to waste any time designing something for a client until you are fairly certain you will get the job. It is not inconceivable that you would design something for them, and then they take your design to someone else and have it made for a lower price. Underhanded, I know, but it can and does happen.

If you fill out a questionnaire during your initial conversations with your client, you can use that information to provide them with a quote for the job. Since you will know what size and what type of materials they need, and can estimate the amount of materials and how many hours it might take you, you can give them a detailed quote for the price and all the other information relating to the job.

For your quote, it is always a good idea to estimate high and then strive to come in under your estimate. This will take into account any unforeseen expenses you might incur and eliminate any bad surprises for your client. It will keep you from having to swallow any expenses that come in over your estimate to avoid having to charge the client for them, which would cause you to lose profits.

ONCE YOU HAVE AN AGREEMENT, IT IS BEST TO REQUIRE A NONREFUNDABLE, GOOD-FAITH DEPOSIT BEFORE YOU BEGIN ANY WORK. Somewhere between 30% and 50% of the total quoted price should guarantee that they really do want you to do this job, and you can then feel safe beginning work on it. You can also use this money to purchase materials for the project, keeping you from having to make a major outlay of money before you can even start. Then, and only then, is it safe for you to finalize the design of their quilt and show them the design for their approval before you begin cutting and stitching.

••• And yes, you can and should charge a design fee for the time you spend designing a quilt just for them. Be sure to build that into your quote.

On the next page is a Sample Quote Form to get you started. Use your completed questionnaire to help you fill it in. Note that on my sample form, I stopped estimating labor costs once the quilt was ready for the longarm, and then I reverted to charging my normal quilting and binding rates for the remaining services needed to finish the quilt. You can do it this way, or simply charge an hourly rate for the entire process, if you prefer.

There is a downloadable version of the Sample Quote Form available (see Downloads, page 10)—so you can print it out as many times as you need to.

✳ YOUR BUSINESS NAME OR LOGO HERE ✳

- - - - - - - - - - - - **CUSTOMER INFORMATION** - - - - - - - - - - - -

Name _____

Street address _____

City _____ State _____ Zip _____

Email _____

Phone_____ Date taken in _____

Date to be completed by_____

- -

QUOTE FOR CREATING A CUSTOM QUILT	PRICE	TOTAL
Quilt top size: _____″ wide × _____″ long		
Design fee: Flat rate, or estimated time required		
Fabric for top: Estimated yardage		
Fabric for back: Estimated yardage		
Making the top, labor: Estimated time required		
Batting: Estimated yardage		
Thread		
Making the back, labor: Estimated time required		
Quilting 　Type of quilting desired 　Square inches: _____″ × _____″ = _____		
Binding: Price for prepping and attaching		
Label		
Any extras required		
Total estimated amount		
Amount of deposit required		

ONCE THE CLIENT HAS APPROVED THE DETAILS, INCLUDING THE PRICE THEY WILL PAY, YOU CAN USE THIS INFORMATION TO CREATE YOUR CONTRACT, WHICH CAN ALSO DOUBLE AS YOUR WORK ORDER. If you are meeting in person, you can have them sign it; if this is a long-distance agreement, you can get their approval in an email and save it.

On the next page is a Sample Contract Worksheet you can use as a starting point. Attach your questionnaire, the approved quote, and any extra information, such as the design layout, to the contract, so you have all the details together in one place.

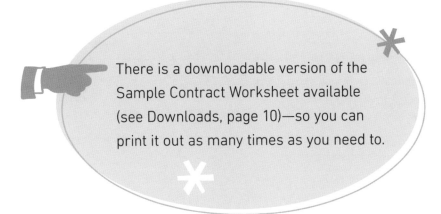

There is a downloadable version of the Sample Contract Worksheet available (see Downloads, page 10)—so you can print it out as many times as you need to.

✳ **YOUR BUSINESS NAME OR LOGO HERE** ✳

-------------- **CUSTOMER INFORMATION** --------------

Name _____

Street address _____

City _____ State _____ Zip _____

Email _____

Phone_____ Date taken in _____

Date to be completed by_____

- -

Quilt description or name _____

_____

Quilt size _____ wide × _____ long

Main colors to be used _____

Fabric swatches

See attached sheet for design of the quilt and any design notes.

Type of quilting desired _____

Thread for quilting _____

Batting _____

Backing _____

Binding_____

Hanging sleeve ⦾ YES ⦾ NO

Label _____

Any special instructions or notes_____

_____

_____

BE AWARE THAT YOUR CONTRACT DOESN'T ONLY PROTECT YOU AS THE MAKER. If you have promised your client to have their quilt done by a certain deadline, it gives them protection in knowing that they will have it when they need it. Both parties are obligated to honor the contract.

Send them progress photos as you work, so they can feel comfortable that you are indeed working on it, and they can approve it as you work, in the event any changes need to be made.

Here's an important word on changes, however:

• • • If a client makes drastic changes to the quilt that will alter the pricing or the time estimated for completion, then you will need to explain this to them. One thing to consider is if you even have time in your schedule to implement the changes they are asking for. If it will add so much time to the job that you can no longer guarantee you'll be done by their deadline, they need to know this.

If the changes cause extra expenses, then make sure they know they will be getting charged more, and make an addendum to your original contract stating what the changes are, and how much more you estimate will need to be added to the price.

CHANGES THAT REDUCE EXPENSES AND TIME INVOLVED CAN SIMPLY BE TAKEN OFF THE ORIGINAL QUOTED PRICE. Possibly, you'll be able to deliver the quilt earlier and under the given estimate, which will only make them an even happier customer.

You need to have a cutoff date for when changes can be made. Some changes will be very difficult to make once the quilt is past a certain point of construction. And once you have it on the quilting frame (or have sent it out to be quilted), changes are really not feasible! I always send at least two progress photos and a photo of the finished quilt top, giving the client one last chance to approve the top before I quilt it, and let them know that no changes can be requested once I've loaded it on the longarm frame for quilting.

Once you have completed the job, you can use the same basic form and outline that your quote uses, but instead plugging in the real numbers now that you have them—you can use this for your final invoice. I also attach copies of any receipts I have for materials I purchased, simply to assure the client that I'm not padding the numbers, and to give them an even more itemized listing of the materials used. Remember to keep copies of all of it for your own records.

Your client may not care to have that much detailed information, but if they ever decide to have a repeat of the item made, all the details can come in really handy. And this can definitely happen. I have made quilts for an entire family, one at a time, all basically the same, and having that information on file saved me a lot of time and effort.

HIRING HELP AND ADDING EQUIPMENT

In Hiring Help (page 155), in Chapter 8, I talked about what you can do to take some of the load off yourself.

If you have more commission work than you can keep up with by yourself, consider hiring employees to help you. You can hire someone to take care of administrative tasks while you sew, or someone to help you with prepping, cutting, piecing, pressing, and binding. You can hire out the quilting part to a longarmer you trust.

NO MATTER WHO YOU HIRE, OR FOR WHAT TASKS, GOOD COMMUNICATION AND PROPER TRAINING ARE IMPORTANT.

> *"I didn't mind training someone because I desired a reliable employee who had a sincere willingness to learn and care for the customer's project."* ~ **MELANIE MILLER-THURNAU, OF SEW & 'TAYLOR' TOO**

If you hire employees, you may need extra equipment or studio space in order for them to be productive. You can't both use the sewing machine at the same time! An extra set of tools, space for them to work, and possibly an extra sewing machine will make their work easier and be more convenient for everyone involved.

If you hire help on a contract basis, then you don't have to pay them regular employee wages or do all the related paperwork, but you likely will have to file a 1099 form for them (if you pay them more than a certain amount in a one-year period). Keep careful records, and check with your accountant, who can help you decide who needs to get the forms—they'll also help you file them.

AN EXTRA-SPECIAL FINISH

Always do your best work, and be proud of the quilts you create for your clients. You're sending them out into the world, and you want to be represented well.

"*You don't want to see a quilt you made a year from now, and ask yourself, 'Did I do that?' Have no regrets.*" ~ KAREN MCTAVISH, OF MCTAVISH QUILTING STUDIO

*

YOU ALSO WANT YOUR CLIENTS TO SAY GOOD THINGS ABOUT YOU AND RECOMMEND YOU TO ALL THEIR FRIENDS AND FAMILY.

It's a kind gesture to show your appreciation to your clients for choosing you to make a quilt for them. In addition to some of the suggestions offered in Personal Touches (page 102), the following are a few ways to make your clients feel special when they receive their finished quilt from you. ●

Sew a "made by" tag on the back. I buy custom-printed sew-in labels from Etsy, with my logo on them, and sew them into the binding on the back of the quilts I make.

Make a label for the back of the quilt that says what the client wants it to say, and sew it onto the back of the quilt. Ink the message on with a Pigma pen, or make the label with your embroidery machine. Making an embroidered label and incorporating it into the backing before quilting is another option.

 Wrap the quilt up nicely for them. Make it a pretty presentation, so they will feel like they're opening a gift. I tie the quilt up with ribbon that I've had printed with my logo, and then wrap it all up in tissue paper that fits my brand.

Include a nice thank-you card with a personalized message. Get some made with your logo on them, or shop for something premade that fits your brand (I found some on Etsy).

Make a matching pillowcase that they can use along with the quilt or use to store the quilt in when it's not in use.

 Of course, you're giving them free domestic shipping if this is not a local delivery, right? That's the least you can do!

you did it!

WHEW! HOW DOES IT FEEL TO HAVE MADE IT ALL THE WAY THROUGH THIS BOOK? I know it was a lot of information to take in, and a lot of hard work, and parts of it probably made your brain ache—but I'm really proud of you for getting this far! Are you ready to start your business?

I hope this handbook has helped you clarify how you're going to go about it. But even more, I hope you will revisit this book every now and then, and use it to recharge, regroup, and make plans to get even better. Looking it all over with more experience behind you may spark some new ideas to help you take your business in an even better direction than you're already headed.

At the very least, it'll be fun to see how your answers to some of the questions have changed since you first started. Just like watching a movie for the second time, you'll invariably notice something you missed the first time around, and it might be just the thing you needed!

I WISH YOU ALL THE BEST WITH YOUR BUSINESS ENDEAVOR—I KNOW YOU CAN DO THIS!

resources

You found it! Those resources I've been referring to throughout the book. Because websites might change over time, if you come across a broken link or path, simply search online. Keep in mind that these are not in any way complete lists because, well, I'd never finish listing. I'm simply providing these as a starting point, and if you need to dig further, the internet is your friend!

BUSINESS START-UP

Internal Revenue Service (IRS): irs.gov

LegalZoom: legalzoom.com; *Especially useful for forming an LLC*

SCORE: score.org

U.S. Small Business Administration (SBA): sba.gov; *Check out the Small Business Development Center (SBDC)—use the locator to find a location near you:* sba.gov > *click* Local Assistance > *click* Search Nearby

Your local Chamber of Commerce

BUSINESS PLAN HELP

APQS Sample Business Plan: *Geared specifically to longarm quilters starting a business:* apqs.com > *under* Education, *click* Business Resources: Start a Business

Internet search: *Search* "How to write a business plan for a small business"*—You will find more information than you can ever use!*

LONGARM MACHINE MANUFACTURERS

A-1 Quilting Machines: a1quiltingmachines.com

APQS: apqs.com

Baby Lock: babylock.com > *click* Our Products > *click* Machines > *scroll to and click* Long Arm Quilting

BERNINA: bernina.com > *click* Longarm Quilting

Eclipse: eclipsequilter.com

Gammill: gammill.com > *click* Shopping? Begin Here > *click* Products

The Grace Company: graceframe.com

Handi Quilter: handiquilter.com > *under* Machines, *click specific machine*

Hinterberg / Nolting: nolting.com

Husqvarna Viking: husqvarnaviking.com > *under* Machines, *click* Long Arm Quilting

Innova: innovalongarm.com > *under* Machines, *click specific machine*

Janome: janome.com > *search* "artistic products" > *scroll to* Content Results, *click* Artistic Products > *click* Long Arm Quilters

JUKI: jukiquilting.com > *under* Products, *click* Quilting Machines

Locksmith Lizzie: locksmithlizzie.com > *click* Products

Martelli: martellinotions.com > *under* Shop All, *click* Martelli Tables > *click* Martelli Longarm and Products

Nolting: nolting.com

Pennywinkle: sunshine16.com

Pfaff: pfaff.com > *under* Machines, *click* Longarm Quilting

Prodigy: gotquilt.com

WHOLESALE THREAD SUPPLIERS

Aurifil: aurifil.com

Fil-Tec: fil-tec.com

Superior Threads: superiorthreads.com

WonderFil Specialty Threads: wonderfil.ca

YLI Threads: ylicorp.com

WHOLESALE BATTING SUPPLIERS

Fairfield: fairfieldworld.com

FiberCo, Inc.: fiberco.com

Hobbs Bonded Fibers: hobbsbatting.com

Mountain Mist: mountainmistcrafts.com

Pellon: pellonprojects.com

Quilters Dream Batting: quiltersdreambatting.com

The Warm Company: warmcompany.com

TOOLS OF THE TRADE

These fine folks all have products to help you do your job better and easier. This list is but a tiny sprinkling of tools available—and new products come on the market nearly every week—so watch social media and favorite quilting websites to find more.

Forever Quilting, Dorie Hruska: forever-quilting.com

Jodi Robinson: jrdesigns.wordpress.com

Kelly Cline: kellyclinequilting.com

Piece N Quilt, Natalia Bonner: piecenquilt.com

The Quilted Pineapple, Linda Hrcka: thequiltedpineapple.com

Quilters Apothecary, Jamie Wallen: quiltersapothecary.com

Quilting Is My Therapy, Angela Walters: quiltingismytherapy.com

Quilts on the Corner, Renae Haddadin: quiltsonthecorner.com

WHERE TO GET PANTOGRAPHS (DIGITAL AND/OR PAPER)

627handworks, Julie Hirt: etsy.com > search 627handworks

Anne Bright Designs: annebrightdesigns.com

Julia Quiltoff: juliaquiltoff.com

Karlee Porter Design: karleeporter.com

Kingsmen Quilting Supply, Inc.: kmquiltingsupply.net

My Creative Stitches: mycreativestitches.net

Quilts Complete: quiltscomplete.com

Sweet Dreams Quilt Studio, Kim Diamond: sweetdreamsquiltstudio.com

TK Quilting & Design II: tkquiltingdesign.com

Urban Elementz: urbanelementz.com

LONGARM QUILTERS (NOTED IN TEXT)

Becky Collis of Collis Country Quilting: facebook.com > search Collis Country Quilting

Ida Larsen of Ida's Custom Quilts: idascustomquilts.com; Check out her online take-in form: idascustomquilts.com > click Pricing > scroll to and click View and Print Order Form

Karen McTavish of McTavish Quilting Studio: mctavishquilting.com

Karyn Dornemann of KarynQuilts: karynquilts.com

Natalia Bonner of Piece N Quilt: piecenquilt.com

CUSTOM QUILTMAKERS (NOTED IN TEXT)

Melanie Miller-Thurnau of Sew & 'Taylor' Too: facebook.com > search Sew & Taylor Too

Victoria Findlay Wolfe of Victoria Findlay Wolfe Quilts: vfwquilts.com

FOR MOTIVATIONAL BUSINESS HELP

Darren Hardy: darrenhardy.com

Marie Forleo: marieforleo.com

Productive Flourishing: productiveflourishing.com

HELPFUL SOFTWARE

You can get specific software tailored for a longarm quilting business, but you can also use other programs that you may already have to do some basic things. That may be enough for you.

TO HELP SPECIFICALLY WITH LONGARM QUILTING BUSINESSES

Machine Quilters Business Manager: eurekadocumentation.com; Specifically geared to longarm quilting businesses. It's got everything in one package: invoicing, supplies inventory, work log, reports, and it can even handle your waiting list!

TO CREATE FORMS OR INVOICES

Adobe InDesign: adobe.com/indesign

Apple Numbers: apple.com/numbers

Apple Pages: apple.com/pages

Microsoft Excel: microsoft.com/excel

Microsoft Word: microsoft.com/word

TO HELP WITH BOOKKEEPING

Apple Numbers: apple.com/numbers

Microsoft Excel: micorosoft.com/excel

QuickBooks: quickbooks.intuit.com

Quicken: quicken.com

MAKING ONLINE COURSES

Coursecraft: coursecraft.net

Craftsy: craftsy.com

Creativebug: creativebug.com

Ruzuku: ruzuku.com

SHIPPING

WHERE TO BUY SUPPLIES

You can buy shipping supplies from your local office, shipping, or postal services store, or online.

I buy a lot of my shipping supplies on Amazon, especially packing tape. It's affordable and so convenient to have them shipped right to my door.

I recycle a lot of cardboard boxes. If something arrives in a box that's the perfect size for shipping a quilt, you can bet I'll be saving it to use for that purpose!

My local printer keeps a supply of empty boxes in the back room, and he lets me rummage through them and pick out some good ones I can use. It saves me money and helps the environment all at the same time!

WHERE TO PURCHASE POSTAGE

Federal Express (FedEx): fedex.com
Purchase mailing supplies, purchase and print shipping labels, schedule pickups, and find drop-off locations.

United Parcel Service (UPS): ups.com
Purchase packaging supplies, purchase and print shipping labels, schedule pickups, and find drop-off locations.

United States Post Office (USPS): usps.com
Purchase postage and mailing supplies, print labels, and track packages.

OTHER STUFF TO CHECK OUT

Facebook: Search for "longarm groups" to find a group that you can join. There you can ask questions, get and give help, and find like-minded quilters.

The Longarm League: If you have a computerized longarm, check out longarmleague.com. It's a membership site for computerized longarm quilters, formed by Jess Zeigler of Threaded Quilting Studio. Membership benefits include a directory to list your business, a lot of business resources, and more.

Longarm University: Longarmuniversity.com has information and education on quilting for hire.

Pinterest: Search to get ideas for setting up your space. Use these phrases to get started:
"longarm quilting thread storage"
"quilt batting storage ideas"
"longarm studio layout"
"sewing studio layout ideas"
If you use those same search terms in a search engine, you will get even more ideas. It's a good time to grab a cuppa and set in to do some planning and dreaming!

Quilting guilds: Search the internet to find a nearby quilting guild dedicated specifically to longarm quilting.

Quilts, Inc.: Visit quilts.com. Produces one public and two trade shows for the quilting and soft crafts industry.

Regional quilt networks or organizations: For a great way to network and promote yourself, check for an organization like this in your area. For example, Heartland Quilt Network (heartlandquiltnetwork.com) is for quilt guilds, quilt shops, and quilting professionals in six Heartland states. Check them out online to see what they offer.

And finally, I hope you'll visit my website Prairie Moon Quilts (prairiemoonquilts.com). You'll find quilting examples and information, tutorials, giveaways, fun activities to join in on, news from the ranch, recipes, news from the studio, organizing challenges, and quilt-alongs. And you can subscribe to get even more information and goodies. I hope to see you there!

about the author

SHELLY PAGLIAI is a quilt pattern designer, author, blogger, coffee lover, ranch wife, goat keeper, cat herder, and professional machine quilter. A quilter since the age of twelve, she started her pattern company in 1999 while working her day job as a computer technician. She started blogging in 2009, and she added a longarm machine to her business that same year. She quickly became so busy with customer quilts that she quit her day job in 2010 to begin designing and quilting full time.

Photo by author

Shelly's work has been featured in numerous quilting magazines, museum exhibits, and books, and has appeared in many major quilt shows, where she has received numerous awards. She is the author of *A Simple Life* (from Kansas City Star Quilts / C&T Publishing).

Shelly quilts on a Nolting Pro Series 24 named "Ivy" in the upstairs of the 1921 farmhouse she shares with her Cowboy at Prairie Moon Ranch in Missouri.

Visit Shelly online and follow on social media!

WEBSITE: **prairiemoonquilts.com**
Check out Shelly's blog among the tabs!

FACEBOOK: **/prairiemoonquilts**

PINTEREST: **/prairiemoonqlts**

INSTAGRAM: **@prairiemoonquilts**

TWITTER: **@prairiemoonqlts**